What Christians Believe

What Christians Believe

by

RICHARD HARRIES

Winston Press, Inc.
430 Oak Grove
Minneapolis, Minnesota 55403

Cover design: Eileen Crowley

Copyright © 1981 by Richard Harries.
Originally published by A.R. Mowbray & Co. Ltd.
in Great Britain under the title *Being a Christian*.
This edition is published by Winston Press, Inc.,
by arrangement with A.R. Mowbray & Co. Ltd.
All rights reserved. No part of this book may be
reproduced in any form without written permission
from the publisher.

Library of Congress Catalog Card Number: 82-050294
ISBN: 0-86683-677-2 (previously ISBN: 0-264-66561-9)

Printed in the United States of America

5   4   3   2   1

Winston Press, Inc.
430 Oak Grove
Minneapolis, MN 55403

For teachers and friends
from good days
at Selwyn College, Cambridge

ACKNOWLEDGEMENTS

I would like to thank Edna and Naomi Capron, Sue Cleland, Helen Oppenheimer, William Purcell, Peter Wheatley and Evelyn Wimbush for reading an earlier draft of this book and making valuable comments from their different points of view. I would also like to thank Sue Cleland for doing the proof-reading and Evelyn Wimbush for doing the typing.

R.D.H.

Contents

Preface

When Evelyn Waugh and Randolph Churchill were on a military mission in Yugoslavia during the last world war they soon found one another's company unbearable. Once, provoked by some outrageous remark, Randolph Churchill blurted out, 'And I thought you were meant to be a Christian and a Catholic,' to which Evelyn Waugh replied, 'And think how much worse I would be if I wasn't'. These pages are written in something of that spirit. The relationship between belief and conduct is a tricky one. This book is written on the following assumptions.

First, belief matters. People sometimes attack what they call the dogma of the Church. But the simplest belief, for example that there is a God, is a dogma, and a religion with no beliefs is an impossibility.

Second, it is possible to have a consistent and coherent view of life. We are battered today by different philosophies and religions. It is easy to think that we cannot choose between them and that one is as good as another. But these conflicting views are not all equally true or valuable. However important it is that we should recognise truth from whatever source it comes, and however sympathetic we are to the idea that truth is multi-faceted, it is both necessary and possible to make up one's own mind on certain essentials.

Third, because I believe the Christian faith to be true I don't thereby think I am any better than anyone else. I expect to see millions of people enter the

Father's kingdom before me, people who have apparently believed little but who have lived truthfully and bravely in response to such light as they had. Whether a person is a believer or not depends on so many factors. For example, if an individual's first contact with the faith is via someone who does not give personal witness to the beliefs he or she professes, or who is cruel, such an experience will set such a strong bias against belief that even having good Christian friends might not overcome it in this life. Further, we are never in a position to know the inner struggles that someone else has had to go through. A genial agnostic might have lost every moral battle. A neurotic Christian might have really tried and won at least one! The only safe course is to follow the Lord's words, 'Judge not,' and to pray that through such faith as we have we may be made better than we would otherwise be.

My hope is that all Christians will recognise here the essentials of the Christian faith clearly set forth. I make no apology for the fact that the beliefs are orthodox. I did not set out to write a book that was orthodox at all costs. It happens that I believe the orthodox Christian faith to be true and, further, I believe it can be seen to be true by all sincere, seeking people. Orthodoxy is its own best advocate, is itself both attractive and persuasive. I hope it can be seen in these pages.

The book is intended to serve three purposes. First, it is a book that can be given to anyone wanting to know what the Christian faith is, what the beliefs are, why they should be held and what the implications are for daily life. Second, it could be used as a study book for adult confirmation classes. Third, it could be used by any group that wanted to examine the fundamentals of Christian faith and their implications for living.

Richard Harries
Fulham, July 1980

1

How do we know God is Real?

John was introduced to Frank at a party and thought to himself, 'I'd like to get to know him.' For this to happen two conditions must be fulfilled. First, Frank must be willing to share something of himself, his thoughts and feelings, with John. If Frank is 'buttoned up', never revealing anything of his real self to anybody, then no one can come to know him. Second, John must be attentive and open to Frank and then willing, in his turn, to put something of himself into the relationship. If every time Frank starts to share some of his real feelings John makes a disparaging remark or changes the conversation to a trivial, safe subject, then there can be no knowing one another. In order for two people to know one another there must be both a willingness to reveal and a receptivity to what is revealed.

The same two conditions apply in knowing God. We cannot know him at all unless he is willing to share his mind and heart with us. We cannot know him at all unless we ourselves are ready to attend to what he discloses of himself, with a receptive and sensitive frame of mind.

Christians, and many other people, would want to say that the first condition has been met. Religious experience of some kind is the almost universal experience of mankind. This experience, however varied, is not just due to human reflection on life. It is the result of the pressure of the divine Spirit on human

1

hearts and minds. It is God trying to make himself known to us. But the way in which we grasp what God is wanting to show us will be coloured by the culture in which we live. And the way that culture interprets it will depend on a number of factors, including the physical geography, the conditions of life of the people, and whether the culture has been shaped by any particularly God-conscious people.

I stood once in a semi-desert in Jordan and felt that there, looking across a hard landscape under a fierce sun, the only God one could worship was Allah. The God of the English, of tidy little gardens and neat hedges, seemed altogether too domesticated. Of course not all English people believe in a tame God. John Donne, William Blake and Gerard Manley Hopkins, to name but three, certainly did not. And there is a tradition within Islam which pictures God as close and loving rather than remote and inscrutable. But the influence of geography is one factor in the ordinary religious experience of mankind. Another is the impact of prophetic souls. The religion of Arabia was transformed by Mohammed. The religion of Sri Lanka was transformed by the Buddha. So although intimations and intuitions of the divine are widespread (and potentially they are open to everyone) the way they are interpreted often differs. The environment, the conditions of life and the cultural tradition all effect the way human experiences of the divine are understood.

If God is real and the God of love that Christians claim him to be, he will want to make himself known to everyone: to some extent he succeeds in doing this. But in addition to this partial but potentially universal disclosure, God has revealed himself in a special way in the life of the people of Israel, from Abraham to Jesus. Our instinctive reaction to this is to say that it's unfair. If God loves everyone equally we cannot allow him to

2

have favourites. But there are two points which put the matter in a rather different perspective. First, there are moments of special disclosure in the lives of many people and these are intimate rather than public occasions. You can know a friend for years, visiting him regularly, and then you discover that, for example, he gives large sums of money each year to charity. You suddenly see the person in a new light. If a person always acts in just the same way to everyone all the time, do we in fact learn anything very much about him? A teacher is, let us say, always scrupulously correct and courteous in dealing with her class. She treats all the children in just the same way, they all know where they are with her, and they all have more or less the same picture of her. But they don't in fact know her very well. Then one day in listening to a child who was very distressed because of her home situation the teacher reveals, because it is appropriate and the knowledge might help the situation, that she has a severely retarded son. Eventually this knowledge gets round the class, and as a result of it the children see their teacher very differently. Respect has grown into something warmer. This example brings out the point that if a person acts in just the same way all the time other people, by the nature of things, cannot know very much about them. They get one picture, which they soon take for granted, and that's all. Further, if there is a special sharing, it is bound to be particular. It was to a particular girl, not to the class as a whole, that the teacher disclosed the fact about her domestic situation. It could have been to the class, but then it would still have been particular in that it wasn't to the whole school. It could no doubt have been to the whole school, or all the schools in an area or a country or a continent. But by then it would have completely lost the character that it had in the beginning. The knowledge that the teacher had a retarded son, when shared in a pastoral situation at just the right moment, was an intimate and powerful revelation. A duplicated sheet from a local authority or a United Nations booklet have a very different character. So, when we come to the deepest things of life, a revelation is bound to be intimate and particular.

The second point is that, as human beings, we are not only very limited in our outlook (having less than an ant's view of the universe) but also our self-centredness darkens the way we see things, including God. In William Golding's novel *The Inheritors*, a contrast is drawn between a group of creatures on the threshold of self-conscious thought and a group who have become fully conscious. The latter have discovered fire, the use of the wind, alcohol and sin. The former have a touching innocence about them. The difference between the groups is also reflected in their religious beliefs. The more primitive group believes in a kind mother earth goddess. The technologically advanced group have a God whom they fear. Left to ourselves our view of the divine is always partial and distorted. Given this situation, if God was going to reveal his true character at all, it was essential for him to do it in a particular way as well as generally through nature and human culture.

The special way God has chosen for revealing his mind and heart to us is in the history of the people of Israel. The important word here is *history*. A person who goes on a continental motoring holiday, perhaps in a car a few years old, perhaps camping, knows how risky life suddenly becomes. You don't know if the car is going to break down. If it does you doubt whether you can get repairs without a long delay. You wonder if you will have an accident. You wonder if the camp site you are making for will be crowded and ghastly. In contrast to one's normal steady routine, every day is an adventure, fraught with the possibilities of good and

4

ill. For the person who believes in God all this experience has a great bearing on their faith. Each day is not just a risk but an act of trust. Each safe arrival in a pleasant spot becomes the occasion not just of heartfelt relief but of thanksgiving. The formative experience of the people of Israel was like this, but much more so. Abraham was called from the place he felt at home in to go out into the unknown. The people of Israel travelled, experienced bondage in Egypt, wandered in the wilderness for forty years, settled in the land they believed was theirs and then went through various other vicissitudes, including captivity in Babylon. The point is that they were primarily a people rather than a country. For much of the time they were a people on the move, forced to trust day by day in the power that had set them travelling in the first place. The result of this experience was that they came to believe in a creative power behind the whole universe and that the character of this power was, above all, one of complete faithfulness. Finally, through all the ups and downs of their existence, they came to a deeper realisation of what this creative mind wanted of them.

It has been said that the Indian sub-continent had no history until its contact with Western civilisation. This doesn't mean that nothing happened. Rather, the Indian experience of life was one of a recurring cycle, with a certain timeless quality about it. So the difference between India (the cradle of Hinduism and Buddhism) and Israel is not that God loves one people more than another. On the contrary, God cares for every Indian soul just as much as he cares for each Hebrew soul. The difference is that the Israelite experience of God was given in and through their experience as a wandering people. This enabled them to apprehend the creative, sustaining power and faithfulness of God in a way which was not possible in a

5

more static society. This does not mean that the Indian experience has nothing to contribute to our understanding of God. It has. It helps to underscore our sense of God's eternity, for example. It stresses, more than the Hebrew tradition, the immortality of the human soul and the possibility of each soul coming in touch with, and living from, God's eternity within us. But God's disclosure of his mind and heart in the slice of human history from Abraham to Jesus is indispensable. From it sprang the great religious traditions of Judaism, Christianity and Islam.

The Jewish people were not chosen because they were God's favourites. Nor was it because they were better than other people. Indeed, their vocation gave them 'an intenser awareness of the reality of sin and its destructive power than other nations'. As they became more aware of the faithfulness of God they became aware also of their own lack of loyalty. As they knew God's blessing when they lived in a right relationship to him, so also they knew the destructive consequences of alienating themselves from the source of their life.

God is poised ready to enter into a relationship with any and every human being. And everyone can experience something of God, enough to respond to him, by reflecting on their own life, particularly their life as a conscious moral being, and the world about them. But for the reasons indicated, God has chosen to reveal himself to us in a special way. We all reveal ourselves more in some actions than others. Disclosure of deep, intimate truths has to take place at the level of the particular rather than the general. Finally, because our innate selfishness tends to make our view of God partial and distorted to a greater or less extent, it was necessary for God to show himself to us as he really is. This he has done in the history of the people of Israel. Through their experience as a wandering people, they

6

discovered a creative power behind the universe that they could trust.

In order to know God two conditions must be fulfilled. God must be willing to reveal himself. He is. And we must be willing to enter into a relationship with him, in particular we must be open to what he shares with us. At this point someone might very well point out that the comparison with getting to know a friend does not work. Before deciding to get to know a human being I know he exists. 'I would like to know God,' we say, 'but I'm extremely doubtful if he exists, and I want to be reassured on that point before committing myself to anything.'

The person to whom I am introduced at the party is there before my eyes. I can see him, hear him, touch him. God is not before me in that physical way. He is an invisible, spiritual, reality. But nor is he a localised presence, as for example a ghost might be to those who believe in such things. For God does not exist as a particular thing. He is the reality in whom we, and all existing things, live and move and have our being. He is not an object in the world of objects, but all objects are contained in him. From him they derive their being, and something of his reality is reflected in them by the very fact that they exist. If we think of a sum of a series of numbers to infinity 1,2,3,4,5,6 . . . etc., God is not any particular number, whether a million, or a million million. He belongs to another order altogether. He is the sum to infinity. Yet something of him shines through each particular number, even the smallest.

In the case of a human being, we distinguish between knowing that a person exists and knowing them as a person. In the case of God, there is another reason, apart from the fact that he is not a localised presence, why this distinction is not so sharp. An implication of what has been said about getting to know another human being is that it is different from getting to know an object. If I am trying to know a stone I stand outside or over it. I can throw it away or pulverise it. But I do not stand outside another person in that kind of way; or if I do I will never know them except as a physical object. Another person is alongside me as an equal. In order to know a person, I have to enter into a relationship which carries responsibilities and in which I might get hurt. In order to know God, not only do I have to be willing to enter into a relationship, another factor is present. God is not just a person alongside me, but my creator and divine lover. I cannot know him unless I have some sense of what it is to be a creature and a willingness to enter into relationship with my creator, with one who, by definition, will make a total difference to my life. I cannot know God unless I am prepared to enter into relationship with a reality whose love for me, if I truly know it, is so intense that it is frightening.

For these two reasons it's not possible, as it were, to produce God and say, 'There he is for you to get to know.' God is not a producible object, not a finite, bounded thing among other finite, bounded things. He is infinite and unbounded. Further, we cannot come to know God in a completely detached and neutral way. We know him, if at all, only as our creator and lover.

REALITY OR WISHFUL THINKING?

What has been said is not meant to detract from the seriousness of the argument against God's existence. It is perfectly proper to want to know that God is real, to have one's doubts allayed. So let us face the lingering suspicions directly. Part of us says that belief in God is manufactured by our need for him. As rational beings we like to have overall explanations of things. Besides, life is hard. So our unconscious, reinforced by the education given in most societies, imagines itself in relation to a God. But it is all wishful thinking. So there are two explanations of our longing for God. According to one, we seek for God because God is real and we are made in his image. According to the other, God is not real and our unconscious throws up the idea of God because it gives us emotional satisfaction. Which of these is true? As has already been said we cannot settle the debate by producing God as a seeable, touchable object. Or, if we did, what we produced would not, by definition, be what Christians, Jews, Muslims and others mean by God. But perhaps there is some rational argument that can convince the non-believer that there is a God?

At least since the time of the ancient Greeks people have put forward proofs for the existence of God. The most popular has been the argument from causality. Nothing happens in life unless something else, or a number of other things, causes it to happen. An avalanche falls because someone dislodged a rock at the top of the mountain (though there are of course innumerable other factors as well). The river flooded because there was four inches of rain last night. To my surprise the supper was already laid, because the children had done it. When we think of the universe as a whole it is natural to think that there must be some cause of it being here, something which corresponds to what we mean by rational, moral purpose. But to say that, because events in this life always have causes there must be a cause of the universe itself, begs the question. It already assumes that what applies in our limited experience is applicable to what is unique and quite outside our experience, the existence of the universe as a whole. So, although it would indeed be satisfying (to most minds) to believe that there is a purposive intelligence which caused the universe to exist, there is no way of proving this. All we can say is that either there is such an intelligence or the universe is self-sufficient. Either there is an uncaused cause (God), responsible for it being here, or it needs no external cause. Logic alone does not enable the neutral observer to decide which of these two views is true.

Another famous and appealing argument is based on the apparent design in nature. When we reflect on the miracle of a flower or a cell or think about the working of the human body or how human life appeared, it is natural to think that some super-being must have designed this. But though it is natural to think like this no proof can be made of it. If I go for a walk through a wood and come across a row of beans, a row of carrots and a row of cabbages growing neatly in carefully turned ground, I assume someone has been at work. This is because I know quite clearly the difference between cultivated and uncultivated ground. I have a standard of comparison. But when we look at the universe as a whole and reflect on the miracle of pattern of which it is composed, we have nothing else with which to compare it. In order to say that the universe was designed by some outside agency we would need to have other universes, some designed and others undesigned, with which to compare this one. But we haven't. This universe is the only one there is. The believer thinks that it has been created and designed by God. The unbeliever does not think this. But again there is no piece of logic which enables the detached observer to decide between these views.

The believer need not be disheartened or in any way lose confidence in the truth of what he believes because of this. The existence of God cannot be disproved either. The so called proofs all leave the matter open.

And, for reasons already suggested, the believer does not find them appropriate ways to know God anyway. For suppose there was a proof which worked, what would we have at the end of it? God is only known when he himself touches the soul of someone, who then responds with delight and longing. It is very possible, it has often happened, that, in reflecting on the origin of the universe or the sheer 'isness' of things, the fact that something, even a grain of sand, exists rather than does not exist, God's grace will touch that person and that person is willing to respond to it. But this is not a paper argument. This is a movement of grace and an answering movement of the soul. Likewise it often happens that a person marvels at some miracle in nature and this deepens their apprehension of God. But this is not an argument from design. It is an open, seeking soul, experiencing something of the miracle of God breaking through the miracle of his world.

To the person who is completely outside faith all this will seem somewhat unsatisfactory. He has been given no logical reason for believing in the existence of God, indeed he has been told that the whole attempt to prove the existence of God is misconceived. His explanation of religion, that it is born of our need and reinforced by social pressures, remains undented. He has been given nothing to justify his making a venture of faith. But there is something that can be said. *Religion is natural to man*. To the believer religion is natural to man because God created us in his own image and our nature is such as to find our ultimate blessedness in relation to him. But the unbeliever can also admit that religion is natural to man without in any way conceding his position. Most people, at every stage in human development, even now, believe in some power behind the universe, usually that there is one creator God. This is a fact. It is also very understandable that, even if such a God does not exist, human beings should give themselves emotional reassurance by projecting the idea of such a God. Even if religious claims are untrue religion seems natural to man.

Whether there is God or not, man needs to believe. He needs to believe that there is a trustworthy power behind the universe.

In fact a useful comparison can be made between the place of trust in human life and the possibility of trusting whatever does or does not lie behind human life. Trust is essential to human community. Unless we can make the basic assumption that most people most of the time can be trusted, there could be no human relationships. Further, if there are no relationships there can be no personality, for we only grow as persons through our relationships with other people. So the basic assumption that people can be trusted is the indispensable condition, not only of human community, but also of the existence of human personality. It is natural to follow on from this and to say that the experience of living as a whole is trustworthy and worthwhile. Without this assumption it is difficult to see that we could go on living at all. The believer says that the experience of living is worthwhile because behind life there is an utterly trustworthy power, a reality who is utterly faithful to us. For, when we use the word God, we always refer to a reality that has a particular character to it. We mean that behind life there is a power that either cares for us, or is hostile or indifferent to us. The believer puts his trust in a caring power behind life and suggests that this is the natural thing to do. This in no way undermines the unbeliever's case but it locates his case against religion at the proper point — the existence of so much suffering and evil in life. It is this which casts doubt upon the existence of a trustworthy power behind life.

In human life we live on the assumption that most people most of the time can be trusted. As a result of bitter experience we come to mistrust some of them. In the same way, it is natural to assume that the experience of living as a whole is to be trusted (that there is a caring power behind life). Hard experience makes us doubt this. For some people life is so bitter that they are forced to deny altogether that there is a divine power that cares. The argument against the truth of religion has to be taken very seriously but it is important to see just what the argument is. The argument is not that God cannot be 'produced', for God by definition is not producible. It is not that the existence of God cannot be proved. For what believers mean by the word God is such that his existence can be neither proved nor disproved. The argument is that, though it is natural for us to believe in a loving God, there cannot in fact be one because life is so bleak and unsatisfactory, full of frustration and tragedy. This argument will be considered in chapter five.

God wills to share himself with every human being. Something of his beauty, power and wisdom break through to us through nature and the ordinary experience of every human culture. But for the reasons given earlier it was not just desirable but essential that God should reveal his mind and heart in a unique way. This he has done in the life of Israel from Abraham to Jesus. In order to enter into a relationship with the true God it is necessary to receive what he has disclosed of himself. Furthermore, we cannot know God in a detached way, as we might know a stone. We can only know God if we are willing to enter into a relationship with one who is our creator and lover. There is no logical reason for taking this step. All we can say is that religion is natural to man and that if we seek God with our whole heart we will find him. The unbeliever says that this 'finding' is an illusion, the result of wishful thinking. But it all depends on what we make of the hard and bitter side of life, whether we think this is compatible with a belief in a loving God. The charge of 'wishful thinking' is, in itself, no argument at all. It amounts to saying that belief in a loving God is too good to be true. But this *assumes* that reality must be bleak and unpleasant. Why should not reality be good? Indeed this is just what the believer says it is. He says that God and the good things which God has in store for us, are beyond our capacity to imagine. We desire such good things, which pass man's understanding, because God has made us like himself and planted a desire for them within us.

SEEKING WITH FELLOW SEEKERS

It is not possible for the convinced sceptic to become a believer by a process of detached reasoning alone. This does not mean that reasoning has no place in the Christian life. On the contrary it is essential. True faith is always, as the greatest Archbishop of Canterbury, Anselm, defined it, faith seeking understanding. It is the nature of genuine faith to try to deepen its understanding of God and his relation to the world. As Cardinal Newman put it, 'faith is the reasoning of a religious heart.' The mind is fully involved at all stages, both in our preliminary searching and in our later desire to know God better; but not the mind in isolation from our will and intuition.

How then do we come to know that God is real? By searching for him; by searching for him with all our heart and all our mind. And genuine faith never ceases to be a searching faith. There is a sense in which our original floundering around for God, even when we are very doubtful, is faith. In the famous words which Pascal put into the mouth of God, 'Comfort yourself, you would not seek me if you had not found me.' But

14

we can never 'find' God without being led at the same time to seek him more ardently, that is, to seek to know him better, love him more and serve him more sincerely. As St. Bernard put it, 'It is thy will, O God, to be found that thou mayest be sought, to be sought that thou mayest the more truly be found.'

Many people reading this chapter will be conscious of their own lack of certainty about God. The times when God has seemed undeniably real will be all too few, the times when he has seemed remote, too many. So the emphasis placed on the necessity of sincerely and ardently seeking God may not be encouraging. Some people have sought God most sincerely and not, apparently, discovered much. But the believer or half-believer or 'I would like to believe' believer is not alone. We may feel that our own awareness of God is almost non-existent but we stand with the community of fellow seekers in our own time and down the ages. No one comes to the faith or deepens his faith on his own. It is usually in company with friends and others whom we meet through their writings. We come to see that a friend has something we would like to have ourselves. We see in a saint something we would like more of for ourselves. Once again, however, it is not as simple as that. Amongst religious believers we are likely to find both those we most admire and those we most dislike. Nevertheless, we would not regard ourself as in any sense a seeker unless we had been able to glimpse something in many believers that we admire and respond to. There is a further point. Many of these believers have gone through long periods of darkness, times when God has seemed almost totally unknown. Yet in retrospect those periods have been seen as times of purification and growth; times indeed when paradoxically God was closer than at any other.

So it does not all rest on our own tiny experience. Anyone who regards himself as a seeker after faith or

15

deeper faith belongs to a fellowship of the spirit which helps to carry us, if we allow it to do so, through the inevitable periods of acute doubt and darkness. But the main point remains. We will come to know God or know him better only if we want to do so.

Questions for discussion

1 Do you agree that all attempts to prove God's existence are misconceived?

2 What times in your life has God seemed most real to you, and why do you think that was?

3 Many, perhaps most, believers go through periods when God has seemed absent or non-existent. What, if anything, has helped to carry you through such times?

4 If God makes himself known, or known better, only to those who sincerely seek him, how in practice should we go about doing this?

2

Who is Jesus?

JESUS AND THE KINGDOM OF GOD

Most people in the West today still believe there must be some divine power that made the universe. It is Jesus that is the difficulty. On any view of the matter Jesus Christ is central to Christianity. But who was he? And who is he for us today? It is not possible, however, to grasp the answers to these questions unless two particular attitudes are already present in the mind.

First there has to be a sensitivity to, and a concern about, the suffering and evil in the world. Second there has to be a belief, or at least, a desire to believe, that there is a loving power behind the universe.

In the Old Testament these two attitudes came together in a particular way. The people of Israel believed in the existence of a creator God and that his nature was above all characterised by faithfulness. But they knew that the presence of so much suffering and brutality in life was a standing contradiction to their belief. So there arose a hope that one day God himself would dramatically intervene in human affairs to overcome all that was evil and bring in a new age. The Old Testament is filled with this hope. It is a longing that suffuses the psalms, the prophets and the historical writings. One day God would act to judge and banish all that was contrary to his will. He would deliver his people and reveal his glory. For in this climax of Israel's history God himself would be disclosed. He would show his hand. Human life, instead of hiding or even contradicting God by its blemishes, would, through its flourishing and blessed state, reveal his underlying presence.

The great longing which arose amongst the people of Israel was not something peculiar to them, that is, of no significance to us now. On the contrary, what they hoped for was only an intenser expression of what will be present in anyone who believes in (or would like to believe in) a loving God and who is aware of the cruel side of life.

It is against the background of this hope that Jesus is to be understood. He proclaimed that the longed-for rule of God in human affairs (the Kingdom of God) was now beginning. Jesus healed people and cast out demons, both signs of the new age. God was present not just in word but in power. 'If I by the finger of God cast out devils, then behold the Kingdom of God is near.' (Luke 11.20.) Jesus invited people to enter this kingdom and taught them what it was to live under the rule of God. This demanded an even more exacting goodness than that practised by the Pharisees, a love that sprang from the heart and knew no limits. A total change of outlook was necessary. 'Repent, the Kingdom of God is at hand.' (Matthew 4.17.) This change was necessary for everyone, religious as well as irreligious, for it meant a switch from an attitude of self-confidence to one of total trust in God.

The message of Jesus was the Kingdom of God. He told people what it was like and said that it was even now breaking into human affairs. In St John's gospel the message seems rather different. There Jesus says amazing things like 'Before Abraham was, I am', and poetical things like 'I am the bread of life'. But St John's gospel is more in the nature of a profound meditation, both devotional and theological, on the total Christian experience, rather than a straight history of the life of Jesus. If we want to know what the Jesus of history said and did, we have to look mainly

18

(though not entirely) to the gospels of Matthew, Mark and Luke (the synoptic Gospels). In the synoptic gospels Jesus did not teach people about *himself* but about *the kingdom*. He used an enigmatic phrase about himself, the Son of Man. This phrase had hints of triumph and glory about it, deriving from the Old Testament and certain writings from the time between the two testaments. 'You will see the Son of Man seated on the right hand of God and coming with the clouds of heaven,' (Mark 14.62) said Jesus at his trial. But Jesus associated the Son of Man with a vocation to suffering. 'The Son of Man will be given up to the chief priests and to the doctors of the law. They will condemn him to death and hand him over to the foreign power. He will be mocked and spat upon, flogged and killed.' (Mark 10.33.)

From this it could be concluded that Jesus was simply the person God had chosen to announce his rule, his coming kingdom. But there are other features of his life and teaching which make that simple solution impossible. First, the authority with which he taught. The clearest example of this is in the Sermon on the Mount (Matthew 5) where we get a series of contrasts, in the form of: 'You have learned that our forefathers were told . . . But what I tell you is this.' It is not surprising that the sermon ends with the comment that the people were astonished because, unlike their own teachers, he taught with a note of authority. Second, there is his claim to forgive sins. Jesus said to the paralysed man, 'My son, your sins are forgiven.' This provoked an immediate response from the religious leaders, 'This is blasphemy! Who but God alone can forgive sins?' (Mark 2.7.) Thirdly, there is the close relationship between what Jesus taught about God's character and the pattern of his own ministry. Jesus gained a reputation as a 'friend of sinners'. He invited everyone including those who, according to

19

Jewish religious law, were failures, to enter the kingdom. He found that the despised and rejected responded more readily to his message than the religiously orthodox, and inevitably he spent time in their company. When challenged about this he taught his sublime parables — the story of the prodigal son and the hard elder brother, the stories of the lost sheep and the lost coin, to mention just three. God, he is saying, is like the father who sees the son in the distance and comes out to meet him; he is like the shepherd who goes over the hills to look for the one sheep who is lost, or the woman who scrabbles all over the floor searching for the lost coin. In other words, what he, Jesus, is doing, going out to those whom others rejected, is what God in his outreaching love always does. The pattern of the one is the pattern of the others. Fourthly, there was the intimate relationship between Jesus and God. He called God 'Abba', Father, a word implying closeness and trust, the word of a young child for his father.

JESUS, CRUCIFIED AND RISEN

It is quite clear that taken singly and together these features presented a challenge to the Judaism of the time. Not just Jesus' message but his person seemed to constitute a threat. We know what happened. Jesus was crucified. The religious authorities felt that he was a blasphemer, one who seemed to set himself over against God's revealed will in the religious law (the Torah) and they arranged for his execution. The full extent of the rejection of Jesus should be measured. He proclaimed the nearness of the kingdom. But the kingdom did not come. Instead, Jesus lay dead. He had taught a distinctive understanding of God as the friend of sinners and a distinctive understanding of goodness. But the sincere interpreters of God's will, as disclosed

20

in the Torah, rejected him. 'Cursed is everyone that dieth on the tree,' said Deuteronomy (21.23). Jesus died the death of a cursed blasphemer, condemned by the Torah to which he had tried to be true.

The full gravity of the crucifixion can be weighed another way. Jesus taught that God was a heavenly Father, 'Abba', one who could be trusted utterly. He believed that God had called him to announce the nearness of the kingdom and to show its incoming power. He had given himself unreservedly to do the Father's will. Was he deluded in believing that God had called him to do this? He must at least have asked the question. Who was he himself? He chose, apparently, the title 'Son of Man' and hinted at a vocation to both suffering and glory. But again, one suspects, it is a question he will have asked himself many times. A person who dives from the high board experiences fear that those who have not let go in that way cannot feel. Jesus trusted completely, he let go utterly into the hands of one whom he believed would be faithful to him. No wonder on the cross he called out, 'My God, My God, why hast thou forsaken me?' So the crucifixion calls into question not only the truth of Jesus' message about the kingdom but the faithfulness of God himself. Jesus gave himself with total loyalty to the one he taught was a loving father. That father seemed to have let him down. Perhaps there is no loving father?

Then on the third day he was raised from the dead. There is an abyss of mystery about the resurrection of Jesus from the dead because it is an event, like the creation of the world out of nothing, that is totally beyond our experience. We can say what it was not, but we can only hint at what it was. It was not simply a change in the minds and hearts of the followers of Jesus so that they saw him in a new way. It is true they did see him in a new way; everything he had said and done was now bathed in a bright light. But this was a result of the resurrection. It is not the resurrection itself. But neither, on the other hand, was the resurrection a simple resuscitation of the dead physical body of Jesus. It was not Jesus coming back to life again in the way he had been alive before. Rather, at the resurrection, Jesus was raised to a new order of life altogether. His dead body was transmuted into the very stuff of eternity. His disciples now knew him as they knew God. If the story of Lazarus is literally true, Lazarus came back as he was before. But Jesus entered a new dimension altogether.

The evidence for the resurrection consists of three parts. First, the finding of the empty tomb. Second, the appearance of the risen Christ to his disciples. Third, the experience of the resurrection power in the Church and our lives now. For the first disciples it was the appearances that were of crucial importance. What is clear from them is that the risen Christ was not, and is not, a localised presence as you and I are. He appeared and disappeared without using the usual doors and stairs. He was at once recognisable and not recognisable. The risen Christ is as God is; a spiritual presence close to all people and all things. But he appeared to his earthly followers as the one they had known on the shores of Galilee and around Jerusalem because that was the way, the only way, in which they could be assured of Jesus' triumphant and glorious life.

Jesus was raised from the dead. His physical body was transfigured into a spiritual body, transmuted into the material of eternity. Henceforth he lives as God lives, present to all people at all times simultaneously. But the first followers had an intense experience of his risen presence associated unmistakably with the Jesus they had known. It was this which made them see Jesus's life and death in a completely new light.

This light, thrown backwards from the resurrection,

reverses the judgement made by men about Jesus. He died the death of the cursed. On the contrary he is most blessed. He was condemned as a blasphemer. On the contrary it is those who crucified him, the Holy one of God, who are the blasphemers. The resurrection is God's unqualified seal of approval of all that Jesus was and stood for. The authority with which he taught, his claim to forgive sins, the identification of his outreach to sinners with God's love for us, his relationship of a son to the Father − all this is revealed to be grounded in God himself. The resurrection does not make these things true. They were always that. But in his ministry they could always be called into question, and on the cross they were denied. The resurrection overthrows the false judgement of men and vindicates Jesus.

The light thrown back by the resurrection also reveals the glory of the earthly life and death of Jesus. The human life of Jesus was one in which his divinity was hidden. He had to struggle and suffer as we do, only more so. He was tempted as we are, only more so. He had no certainty about the validity of his mission or any final understanding about who he was. His life was a fully human life. The resurrection reveals it to be a divine life − lived out under human conditions. No wonder when the gospel writers came to put down their story, they could hardly refrain from seeing some of that glory already there, apparent to the eyes of the disciples as they listened to Jesus. How sublime of the writer of the Fourth Gospel to see the whole ministry of Jesus as a manifestation of divine glory, one which came to its climax on the cross. For the author of the Fourth Gospel especially, everything was suffused with the resurrection, and the cross was in no sense a defeat but a glorious victory, a supreme revelation of the divine glory. And so it was. Only that is not how it seemed at the time. At the time Jesus experienced dereliction.

The hope of the Old Testament was that God himself would decisively intervene in human affairs to overcome all that was contrary to his will of love. In his ministry Jesus began this process, the sick were healed, demons were cast out and the poor had good news preached to them. Yet, as is all too apparent, suffering and evil continue unabated. How can Jesus be said to have overcome evil? If, as D. H. Lawrence put it in one of his poems, 'All that matters is to be at one with the living God,' then evil is nothing less and nothing more than separation from God. Jesus lived a life of complete unity with his heavenly father. It was a life of total trust and filial response to the Father's good will for him. Furthermore, it was a trust tested by the most severe conditions. He went into the darkness of human sin. He was condemned as a blasphemer, he died the death of one cursed by God. Yet through all this, despite apparent despair, he was not alienated by sin from the Father. At one point anyway evil has been finally conquered, and that is in the life of Jesus himself. He lived out his life in a totally human way under the conditions of sinful human existence with an unbroken unity with the father. In him there has been a decisive victory over evil. But Jesus though he lived the life of a particular person, is now a universal spiritual presence. Through association with him the sin in our life and the evil in our surroundings can be pushed back. He lived a life of unbroken unity with the Father and through our relationship to him nothing can separate us from the Father either, even our own sin. For we are joined by faith and baptism to Christ and, in the words of a hymn, the Father only looks on us as found in him. Through being born and brought up in a far from perfect environment and through our own wrong choices we are, whether we are aware of it or not, alienated from God. We, just as much as the people who physically condemned and crucified Jesus, are revealed to be blasphemers. But we don't have to experience the darkness of total alienation from God, because Jesus has entered this darkness on our behalf. This darkness is not a punishment which God inflicts. It is the logical and inevitable consequence of sinful human choices. But Christ underwent this for us and, through association with him, we no longer have to suffer the alienating consequence of our sin. For, as Paul put it, nothing can separate us from the love of God in Christ.

In Jesus the hope of the Old Testament was fulfilled. In him God acted to overcome evil. In him the glory of God is revealed. Thus it was that after the resurrection the message of Christians was not the kingdom of God but Christ. Jesus proclaimed that the kingdom of God was breaking into human history. The first Christians believed that in a decisive sense it had come in the person of Jesus. In him the will of the Father was perfectly accomplished. In him the back of human sin was broken. In him God himself was revealed. So Christ himself, rather than the kingdom of God is the theme of Christian preaching.

The resurrection reveals that in Jesus God himself is encountered. More precisely, the intimate relationship of a son to a heavenly Father, which was so distinctive of Jesus, and which was the heart of his ministry, is revealed to be an eternal relationship. Jesus lived his life from the Father and to the Father. All that he was and did came to him from God and his whole life was a response to the Father's good purpose for him. The resurrection reveals this to be a working out in human terms of a relationship which is eternal. He is not just a human being called into a close relationship of sonship to the heavenly father, but the eternal Son of God living an incarnate life.

We are now in a position to answer the question 'Who is Jesus?' He is the Christ, the Son of God. The word Christ is the Greek word for Messiah. Although it is unlikely that Jesus used the word about himself because of all the false connotations it had in people's minds, the Christian Church has always used it to signify the important truth that Jesus fulfilled the hopes of the Old Testament. He is the one in whom God acted to overcome sin and bring in God's rule on earth. In doing this he reveals God and shows himself to be the Son of God.

It was suggested in the last chapter that if God was going to disclose himself to us at all it was necessary for there to be, not only a general disclosure of himself to all people in all cultures, but a particular revelation. Various reasons were suggested for this, for example the fact that our normal view of God is conditioned by our environment and warped by our limited and sinful outlook. Furthermore, for the disclosure of deep truths it is necessary for there to be an intimate and personal setting. Reasons were also suggested why this particular self discipline by God should have been in the life of the Jewish people, rather than on the Indian sub-continent. This sharing by God of his heart, mind and purpose for us, which began with Abraham, comes to its climax and consummation in Jesus. He is the eternal Son of God revealed in human terms. The whole of the Old Testament, indeed the whole evolution of mankind, was a preparation for this.

HOW CAN WE BELIEVE?

Jesus is the Christ, the fulfiller of the hopes of the Old Testament. He is also the incarnate Son of God. But how can a person today come to believe something as astounding as this? There is a phrase in one of Cardinal Newman's sermons which provides a hint. Newman wrote of 'the blessedness of a mind that believes readily'. The immediate and natural reaction to this statement is the assertion of its contrary, 'How dangerous is a mind that believes readily.' A mind that believes readily can believe all manner of superstition and falsehood. A mind that believes readily could also be called credulous or gullible. Better by far, we think, to be tough minded and sceptical, critical of everything that we are called upon to believe. But this, at least, in favour of Newman's assertion can be said. It is not reprehensible to *want* to believe that there is a loving power behind human life. It is not reprehensible to *want* to believe that evil can be finally overcome. Indeed someone who does not want such things must be a little strange.

Imagine for a moment that the Christian gospel is true. Pretend, if you like, that there is a loving God who made you; he made you a bit like himself and with the potential to become quite godlike. Pretend that this God was born as a man to overcome evil and reveal himself fully. That he wishes to unite himself to you and raise you into eternal life, a life from which nothing can take away and which lasts for ever. Pretend all this and admit perhaps that, if it were true, the God who made you would also have filled you with a longing for such blessedness, a longing which would not be satisfied with anything less than this. For, if it is true, how can we know such a God without a great longing? So God implants in human hearts a restlessness which makes us finally dissatisfied with all human goods, and which leads us on until it recognises the supreme gift of himself to us in Christ.

Jews, Christians and Muslims are agreed that there is one God, maker of heaven and earth and that we only know this God because he has chosen in his mercy to reveal himself to us. Jews believe the revelation stops short of Jesus, that God's will and purpose for us is made known in the Torah, the holy law. Muslims believe that the revelation continues past Jesus to Mohammed and that God's will and purpose for us is made known in the Koran. How are we to choose between these three, all of which claim to be God's disclosure of himself? There is no neutral ground on which we can stand and say, 'Yes, that is from God and that is not.' For such a judgement presupposes that we already know what is of God and what is not. But we only know what is of God in so far as he has revealed it to us, and that is just the question. Where has he revealed himself? So there is no detached, rational way of discriminating between these three claims to be God's disclosure of himself to us. But this at least can be admitted. No better news than the Christian story is imaginable. Jews believe that God has revealed his nature in a book and a tradition. Muslims believe he has revealed it through a book and Mohammed. Christians believe that he himself, in the form of his eternal Son, has come amongst us, to die, rise again and unite us to himself. Call it a fairy story − but a sublime one. Call it unbelievable − but unrivalled in its haunting beauty. Christians believe that there is a longing in the human heart that will not be satisfied by anything less lovely than this, because this is in fact what God is like.

It is still open to the sceptic to give an alternative explanation to this longing: it is wishful thinking. But although this is an alternative explanation which can never be refuted it cannot be proved right either. As was pointed out in the last chapter it rests on the assumption that the Christian understanding of God is too good to be true. But this is an assumption, not something that can be argued for on rational grounds. The Christian says about his or her faith: 'It is good − and it is also true.' The sceptic may suggest that those who are looking for a God of love are compensating for a lack of love in their own life; those who are looking for a God of tenderness are making up for the fact that they feel crushed and broken by life; those who are looking for a God of forgiveness are prompted by irrational feelings of guilt. Some of this may be true. Indeed it would be surprising if it were not. For according to the witness of the biblical writers it is the humble and broken in heart who are most able to believe. It is complacency, self-satisfaction, cockiness of all kinds that cuts us off from God. Very often it is the death of someone much loved, or even a marriage breakup that is the occasion for a person being more open to the gospel than they ever were before. This is not the compensation of a divine love for a human one. It is the opening of the heart to receive a divine love that was there all the time, in part expressed through the human love, but which we were not able to receive in our fullness. In our emptiness, in our need, our poverty, we turn to receive from him whom we have shut out in our plenty. So it is that those who have been most crushed or broken by life, those who have discovered the power of sin within themselves or who have been disillusioned by secular attempts to overcome evil, are open to the gospel in a way which those who are superficially strong and self-confident are not.

In Christ God has conquered evil. Yet evil continues rampant. Human beings still sin and suffer. This seems to undermine the Christian claim. But the Christian claim is not just that Christ has died and risen, it is that he will come again in glory. The acclamation at the Eucharist is: 'Christ has died. Christ is risen. Christ will come again.' Christ's resurrection was the beginning of the new age. In him the kingdom of God came in some decisive way. But we live in between the times, between the beginning and the consummation. We cannot yet see evil eliminated. We do not see Christ in glory.

What we can do is discover his presence and power in our own lives now. The God who raised Jesus from the dead and who will recreate us anew for eternity can be known now, raising us out of sin and despair into new life. Belief in Christ's resurrection does not depend entirely on the witness of the first disciples to their encounter with him. It is also based upon the power of his resurrection now. Through our relationship with Christ, through allowing him to take hold of us and permeate us through and through, the divine life revealed in him can shine in us as well.

There are two serious arguments against the truth of the Christian claim. The first is the extent of human suffering, which will be considered in chapter five. The second is the persistence of sin within ourselves and the Christian community. For the Christian claim is that we can know something of the power of the resurrection now to overcome sin. Those outside the Church do not always find this. Too often they see a quality of life which is petty and drab, dejected and meanminded. In so far as they see correctly and do not exaggerate the goodness of life outside Christ the criticism is, rightly, undermining of Christian belief. For although we cannot base the truth of beliefs upon human experiences, nevertheless, the importance of experience as a touchstone of belief cannot be ignored. For the believer himself, 'Taste and see that the Lord is good' is crucial. He finds through faith, prayer, the Christian fellowship and the attempt to be a follower of Christ, a way of living life which is satisfying. The unbeliever does not have that experience, but he looks at the Christian and the Christian community to examine the fruits of what they believe. Sometimes he finds those fruits edible and sometimes he finds them nauseous. We live between Christ's resurrection and his coming again in glory. During this time the credibility of what Christians believe about the past and what they hope for the future, depends, in large measure, on the quality and authenticity of their lives now.

The Christian faith was first preached as 'Good News'. It is still good news, despite the stale or distorted way it has often been presented, because it answers the deepest longings of the human heart. There can be no better news than that behind human life there is a power of love. This love has revealed his heart and mind to us in Jesus, who through his death and resurrection, has broken the back of evil. This Jesus is the eternal Son of God, made man. We can relate to him and associate with him. We can live in him and allow him to live in us.

Questions for discussion

1   This chapter has emphasised the centrality of the resurrection of Jesus from the dead. If you came to disbelieve this (or if you came to believe it after having previously denied it) how would this change your attitude to life?

2   In what sense, if at all, can we say that the decisive victory over evil has been won through the life, death and resurrection of Jesus?

3   How do you counter the charge that belief in a God of love, particularly a God who for love of us was born as a man, is wishful thinking?

4   Many of the first hearers experienced the gospel as 'Good News.' Why today do so many find it stale, dull and even anti-human?

3

Father, Son and Holy Spirit

FATHER

When the question 'Who is Jesus?' has been answered, the ground is clear to consider the Christian understanding of God as Father, Son and Holy Spirit. Every Sunday believers say:

> 'We believe in one God,
> The Father, the Almighty,
> maker of heaven and earth,
> of all that is seen and unseen.

Scientists today speculate on whether the universe began at a single point millions and millions of years ago (the so-called 'big bang' theory) or whether matter is being created all the time (the so-called 'little pop' theory). Both acounts are compatible with the belief that God is maker of heaven and earth. For, by whatever process matter comes into being, God is the ultimate cause of it. God himself is uncreated. He simply *is*. He always has been and he always will be; and he himself is responsible for everything that exists (except evil). Moment by moment he holds it in being. When we think about God as creator we are not so much concerned with what might have happened millions of years ago but with the fact that God is the creative source of all that exists now. When we look at something, however small, a grain of sand or a speck of dust, we can reflect that it might not exist. But it does exist. There it is. Besides its particular colour and shape there is its sheer 'isness'. It might not have existed but it does exist. The fact that it exists is due to the uncreated creator, the uncaused cause, of all particular existences.

It is sometimes stressed that God creates 'out of nothing'. When human beings make something they have materials to work on. The sculptor has stone, the carpenter has wood. But there are no pre-existent materials for God to work on. They only exist if he creates them 'out of nothing'. This is impossible for us to imagine. Yet, when we are, as we say, being 'creative' there is a faint clue to what is meant. When we are creative we get an idea that is not just a repetition of what someone else has thought. We could not, for example have predicted that given some paint, a canvas and a view, Constable would have painted a picture in a particular way. When we are creative a genuinely new element is present. The idea, we say 'came out of the blue'. But it did not. It came out of us. Yet it was still new. Something came that was not there before. So God creates out of himself, not just ideas but a whole universe. Out of love God conceives the idea of making free creatures: and for him the idea and its execution are simultaneous.

The fact that we have scientific accounts of the origin of the universe on the one hand and a belief that God is maker of heaven and earth on the other poses a question about the relation between these viewpoints. They are not antagonistic to one another but complementary. The scientist and a person thinking about the meaning of life (whether he is a scientist or anyone else) are asking different questions. The scientist asks questions like, 'How did this come about?' and his answer is some kind of description. When we are thinking about the mystery of the universe we ask questions like, 'Why does anything exist and what is the meaning of it all?' The answer, if there is one, is not a description. As you read this page a person trained to understand the way the brain works can ask what is happening and the answer will be a complicated one about the way the eyes and the brain function. But if the question asked is 'Why are you reading,' this is not a question that wants a descriptive or scientific answer. The answer will be something like 'I want to deepen my understanding of the Christian faith' or perhaps 'I just wanted to read'. It is an answer in terms of personal purpose. So when we ask a question like 'Why does anything exist and what is the meaning of it all.' scientific accounts about the origin of the universe are no help at all. They are equivalent to descriptions of how the brain and eye work. Appropriate answers are 'God created it out of his love' or 'I can find no answer to that question' or 'An evil being created it to torment others.' Scientific answers about the origin of the universe, fascinating though they might be, do not impinge on what the opening chapters of Genesis are about. They say, in story form, that all things depend for their existence upon God. Current scientific theory favours some version of the 'big bang' theory but, whether it is true or not, the Christian faith is concerned with something more fundamental, the ultimate dependence of all things upon an uncreated power beyond the universe. For reasons given in the first chapter this power cannot be treated as a describable object. But it, or rather he, can be known by the loving heart willing to live with a sense of creaturely dependence.

The distinction between scientific and religious questions applies equally to the theory of evolution. Whether the theory of evolution is true is a matter for those competent in that particular field of scientific work to decide. As a matter of fact most modern scientists do think it is true. Further, most religious minded people find that it deepens their belief in God as creator rather than undermines it. In the light of evolution, creation is seen as a continuing process leading to a great climax. First matter, then life, then conscious life, then Christ, then in the end all people and all things made like Christ. Creation is continuing now. God did not just wind the universe up and let it go. Moment by moment he not only holds it in being but also shapes it. He shapes it through the laws of nature, the stable, chemical, biological and atomic processes that take place. He also shapes it through the interaction of his spirit and our free spirits. It is possible also that there is something corresponding to our consciousness all the way back through evolution, so that there is some rudimentary interaction of divine spirit and finite inner life in creatures lower down the evolutionary scale than man and that this has played a part in the evolutionary process. But whether this is true or not creation is a continuous process in which God is involved at every level — atomic, molecular, cellular and conscious.

Everything that exists is utterly dependent for its being on a divine power. For people brought up to believe in the importance of self-reliance this stress on the ultimate dependence of all things on God can create difficulties. Maturity involves becoming independent of our parents and standing on our own feet. But there are many ways in which, whether we like it or not, we remain dependent on others; and to acknowledge this is not immaturity but realism. We are dependent on the air we breathe and the blood in our veins. We are dependent on all those whose work provides what we need. We are dependent on the love and respect of others — and often their advice and wisdom as well. This realisation of our dependence on others, just as much as an assertion of our personal responsibility, is the mark of a mature person. The same applies in our relation to God. Maturity involves both an assertion of our personal responsibility and an acknowledgement that, every second, we depend for our sheer existence, as well as for all that is good in us, on him.

The Christian understanding of God as Father/creator has important practical implications. Because God is the creator of the physical universe it is essentially good. Some religions have taught that matter is evil and that being religious means trying to become more and more detached from all things physical. This is not the Christian understanding nor the Jewish or Islamic. God is the one creative source of all there is, so all that exists is in essence good. The implications of this are first that physical things can be enjoyed. Trees and mountains, lakes and oceans, fresh air and fresh fruit, the bodies of those we love and our own bodies as they love us, are given us for our pleasure and delight. Second, the physical conditions under which people live matter. Christianity can never be a matter of helping people grow spiritually or morally while remaining indifferent to their material well being. Third, because God is the creator of material things they can be used in a special way to unite us to himself. They can become sacraments. These three points will be explored further in later chapters.

The Jews believed that the power which was shaping their life and the power that brought the universe into being in the first place, was good. He was a God of loving kindness; a God who was faithful to them. They felt life to be a blessing and they blessed the one who gave it to them. So when Jesus calls God 'Father', he is not saying anything new. The Father whom he trusted utterly and to whom he gave his allegiance is the loving wisdom and almighty power whom generations of Jews before him had known. Yet, as scholars have pointed out, what is new is the use of 'Abba', the child's word expressing intimacy and trust. The one who gives me my being is not just a creator but a father, an Abba; one who is close to me and whom I can trust utterly.

SON

The previous chapter described how Christians came to believe that Jesus is the eternal Son of God made man and gave reasons for thinking this faith still holds true. In the first centuries of the Christian era, when believers were being put to death for their faith, they were forced to think hard about God and Jesus. Some people suggested, for example, that, though the Son of God is divine he is not quite fully God: that at some point, long before the origin of the universe, there was a time when the Son of God did not exist. Under the guidance of the Holy Spirit and over a long period, amidst much confusion, when the issues did not always seem as clear as they do to us, the Church rejected this way of thinking. They affirmed that the Son of God was fully God, one in his very essence or being with the Father. This discussion resulted in the Nicene Creed (from the Council of Nicaea held in 325 — though the Creed was not fully formulated until the Council of Constantinople in 381).

The words are:

> 'We believe in one Lord, Jesus Christ,
> the only Son of God,
> eternally begotten of the Father
> God from God, Light from Light,
> true God from true God, begotten, not made,
> one in Being with the Father,
> Through him all things were made.'

Those who argued for this belief put forward a number of reasons, but the heart of the matter was that only God himself could redeem us. If God wanted to unite us to himself and make us Godlike, only he himself could do this. Christians knew in their own experience how Christ had united them with the Father, and they could only believe that it was God himself, in Christ, bringing this about.

But the same kind of argument, only if Christ were fully God could he redeem us, applied to the humanity of Jesus as well. Only if he was truly human, could our humanity be redeemed. Some people thought that Jesus was the Son of God going about in a human body. But this is no help. For it is not so much our body but our minds and wills which lead us astray. Only if Jesus had a mind and will like ours could he be of use to us. So as the Church affirmed that Jesus was truly God, so they affirmed just as strongly that he was truly human. This of course raised the further question of how the divine and human side of Christ are related? He might appear to be a hybrid. But the Church decided that Christ is one true person just as we are. The Council of Chalcedon in 451 asserted not only that Christ is truly God and truly man but that the divine and human natures in him both remain distinct and yet come together to form one true person.

Our forebears in the faith felt that only some such statement could do justice to the evidence of the New Testament and their own experience of salvation in Christ. But can anything else be said to help us understand this truth? Many attempts have been made down the centuries, not least in the last two hundred years, to understand how Christ could be both human and divine. The most popular in recent years has started off from the experience of God's inspiration and help in our lives (grace). It is sometimes our experience to ask for God's strength to carry out some difficult task, which we know is our duty, and to receive that help. Two things are discovered. We ourselves have to try hard. But it seems as though it is God's help that enables us to succeed. Not a bit of us and a bit of God but an overlapping of the two. A good action is at the same time God's and ours. This was the experience of St. Paul who wrote: 'But by the grace of God I am what I am, and his grace to me was not without effect. No, I worked harder than all of them — yet not I, but the grace of God that was with me.' (1 Corinthians 15.10.)

This is a hint of how the divine and human can both be present at the same time. If we use this as a picture of Christ we can say that in him the interpenetration of the divine and human is complete; there is a perfect union. Yet the experience of God's grace in our lives is only a clue to the union of the divine and the human in Christ. That union is not simply what we know in our own experience carried to its limit. It is something beyond our experience, something beyond the limit of what we can understand. For in the end we have to say it was not just God's grace that was present in Jesus, but the Son of God himself. Whenever we talk about God we get into difficulties and no more so than here. To talk at all we have to take something with which we are familiar. But to talk about God (as opposed to a God made in our own image) we have in the end to point to what is outside our own experience. If we begin with the experience of grace in our lives it can only be as a clue to point to what is beyond our grasp, to what has no parallel, the union of the eternal Son of God with a human life.

These considerations, though they may sound theoretical, are crucial to Christian truth, for God was in Christ, leading a human life like ours, in order to unite us to himself and take us into eternal life. This divine incarnation (enfleshing) is the supreme act of divine humility. God emptied himself to become as vulnerable to the slings and arrows of outrageous fortune as any human being. From the beginning God pours himself into his creation. From the beginning he makes himself vulnerable by making a universe which can hurt him. From the beginning he puts all he is into the universe. So the incarnation is congruous with, of the same character as, the creation of the universe — it is an outpouring of love, an act of humility. But it is not just the supreme instance of what God always does. It is a unique, never to be repeated act. God always enters imaginatively into our situation and feels what we feel, for his love is unlimited, boundless, omnipresent. But in the incarnation he goes beyond even this. The Son of God actually unites himself to human nature, becoming as vulnerable as a babe. He lets go to the extent of entering the fragile canoe of human nature, and shooting the rapids of perilous human existence. Father Damien in the nineteenth century went to live on a leper island, knowing what it would entail. One day he began his sermon to the lepers in the church he had helped them to build, 'Now I too am one of you.' In Christ God says to us, 'Now I too am one of you.'

In Jesus the external Son of God enters fully into the sin and sorrow of human existence to the extent of becoming one of us. This is not only that we may have a God who understands us fully. It is that we ourselves may be joined to God, the sin in us being overcome. Through Christ's ascension triumphant human nature is taken into heaven. This means that the union of God and man in Jesus is an eternal one. The Son of God did not take our nature to be put off at the end of the day like a suit of clothes. In Christ God and men, heaven and earth, are joined never to be unjoined. This is of the utmost importance for us. It means that because, through faith in Christ, we are joined to him, we too are raised to the life of heaven. Through putting our trust in the Son of God we become 'in Christ'. In other words Christ becomes for us not only a person to whom we can pray, but a reality in whom we are incorporated. We are taken into the very life of the Godhead. In Christ God and man are united never to be separated. In him human nature is taken into God. Through faith in Jesus as the Son of God we are joined to him in such an intimate way that we become in Christ. Being in Christ we ourselves are taken into the life of the Godhead. That is why these difficult questions discussed by the first Christians are not obscure irrelevancies. They are crucial. It is only because God himself is in Jesus, and because Jesus is a man as we are, that we can say that through being joined to him we are taken right into the very life of the Godhead.

SPIRIT

In the story of Christ's baptism a voice was heard from heaven 'Thou art my Son, my Beloved; on thee my favour rests.' The voice was the voice of God. It was addressed to Jesus as his Son. But there is also a third reality present. 'Heaven opened and the Holy Spirit descended on him in bodily form like a dove.' When Christians read this story they see here a picture of the Trinity. Jesus, the Son of God, prays to his Father and between them flows an unbroken cycle of love. So if we ask who or what is the Holy Spirit, the answer is 'The Holy Spirit is the love which flows between the Father and the Son.' This love overflows to create the world. At the creation 'the Spirit of God was moving over the face of the waters' (Genesis 1.2). The same spirit is present in the life of the people of Israel guiding, teaching and inspiring them. Nevertheless, from the time of the exile in Babylon in the sixth century BC, the Jews looked forward to a new age of the Spirit, to the time when the Spirit of God would be poured out to renew human life. In the New Testament Jesus is depicted as a man filled with the Spirit who is bringing in the new age of the Spirit.

After the death and resurrection of Jesus the first Christians experienced such an outpouring of the Spirit that they were convinced that this new age had indeed begun. In the fourth and fifth centuries, after the Church had clarified its understanding of the Son of God, they did the same for the Holy Spirit. They affirmed that the Holy Spirit was no less fully God than the Son. So the creed puts it:

> 'We believe in the Holy Spirit, the Lord, the giver of life,
> who proceeds from the Father and the Son.
> With the Father and the Son he is worshipped and glorified.
> He has spoken through the Prophets.'

There are three reasons for saying that the Holy Spirit is divine, all of practical significance. First, when people become believers they are usually convinced that, even before they took this step, the Holy Spirit was present in their lives leading them into the way of truth. Second, the same conviction arises about the process whereby a person comes to recognise God in Christ. Only what is itself of God can recognise God. It is God within us, the Holy Spirit, that enables us first to recognise and then respond to God's disclosure of himself in Jesus. Third, it is the Christian experience that every aspect of the Christian life from prayer to martyrdom is inspired, sustained and developed through the Holy Spirit within us. As Paul puts it about our prayers, 'Likewise the Spirit helps us in our weakness; for we do not know how to pray as we ought, but the Spirit himself intercedes for us with sighs too deep for words. And he who searches the hearts of men knows what is the mind of the Spirit, because the Spirit intercedes for the saints according to the will of God.'

(Romans 8.26.) In short when we search for faith it is God within us seeking God. When we come to recognise God in Christ, it is the God within us recognising God beside us as our brother. When we try to live the Christian life of love and prayer it is God within us living the God-life through us. This God within us is the Holy Spirit.

What is the relationship between the Spirit at work in the length and breadth of creation and the great outpouring of the Spirit that took place at the first Pentecost? Christ was, as it were, filled to the brim by the Holy Spirit. This was because he lived a life of total trust in the Father. But he does not hug this relationship to himself. He came to share it with us, to bring us into the same relationship of son and heavenly Father that is his eternally. As we come to have that relationship the cycle of love that flows between the Father and the Son comes to flow in and through us. So it is that Jesus is not just a man filled by the Spirit. He brings in the age of the Spirit. He draws people into such a relationship with his Father that they too become filled with the Spirit that filled him. Within everyone, whoever they are, the Spirit is present, ready to well up. And because no one is totally depraved (there is honour even amongst thieves) the Spirit manages to seep into every life. But it is only when a person has been taken into Christ's relationship with the Father that the Spirit is actually allowed to well up. This is what happened on the first Whitsun and this is what happens every time a person is brought into a true relationship with God through Christ. So the Holy Spirit is the Spirit of Jesus, released by his cross and resurrection, for it is through these events that a person is brought into a relationship with the Father which nothing can break.

What about the different roles of the Spirit within us and Christ? The relationship has been depicted in a number of ways. Perhaps the most helpful is still that which thinks of Christ being formed in us or of us being made like Christ, with the Spirit being the agent of this, the quickening power that brings it about. So although it is our relationship with Christ that allows the Spirit to take hold on us; it is the Spirit that enables us first to respond to Christ and then to become like him. For only the Holy Spirit, God himself, could form us into Christ.

For a person who is already a Christian the Holy Spirit is not just important as the one who deepens our understanding of God and who enables us to love God and one another more. He gives us specific gifts. Every Christian is given a gift of the Holy Spirit, enabling him to reveal the glory of God in Christ. This gift is closely related to the kind of person we are, about which more is said in chapter nine.

THREE PERSONS IN ONE GOD

The pressure of their experience led Christians both in the New Testament period and after to affirm, first, that the Son of God is truly and fully God and, then, that the Holy Spirit is no less truly and fully God. But Christians believe, no less strongly than Jews and Muslims, that God is one. How can God be three persons in one God? This question has caused more difficulty than it ought. The fact is that personality is a social reality. We only become persons through relationships with other persons. We are familiar with the sight of adults bending over a pram and talking to a baby who has not yet begun to talk. Through being talked to the baby will eventually learn to talk back; and through learning to talk will come to think; and through coming to think will begin to grow into a person. There is no such thing as a completely isolated person. Even the hermit was once a baby who through

44

his relationships with persons came himself to think, talk and pray. So in saying that there are three persons in one Godhead the Christian faith is not asserting anything contradictory to reason. There is relationship within the Godhead and this is entirely congruous with what we know from our own experience of personality. Personality and relationship are inseparable.

We can even go further than this. When two people achieve a loving relationship they become aware of a profound unity. Married couples sometimes speak half jokingly of 'my other half' and, more seriously, when a partner has died, of 'being cut in half'. But this unity does not lead to any diminution of their own personality. On the contrary, the deeper the unity the richer and more flourishing does each individual personality become. Within God the unity is profounder and the persons more distinctive than anything we know in human life; but loving relationships give us some clue as to what is present, to an infinite degree within God. The same truth can be explored in terms of our relationship with God himself. A deep relationship with God does not lead to the obliteration of our own personality. Just the opposite. The closer the relationship, the deeper and richer becomes the personality. The profounder the unity, the more I am I.

The Christian understanding of God is that he is best characterised by saying that there are three persons within the one Godhead. When the first Christians used the word person, however, they did not mean self-conscious personality, as we do now; so some prefer to use the phrase 'mode of being'. Either way, the picture of God is of the divine Father, the source of all being, eternally pouring himself out to his Son; the Son making a perfect response of trust and obedience; and the Holy Spirit, the bond of love, flowing between them in an eternal cycle. The portrait we have of Jesus in the Gospels — as one who gave himself completely to the one he called Abba, Father, and being enabled to do this by the power of the Holy Spirit within him, is a revelation in human terms of what is true eternally. In the Gospels we have a slice of the eternal Godhead. To put it the other way round, the eternal Godhead is revealed in human terms.

The first implication of this Trinitarian faith is that God is complete in himself. He has no unmet needs. He does not create the world because he is lonely, but out of the fullness of his being. God is complete and self-sufficient in himself but this does not mean he is invulnerable. A family with two children might decide to adopt another. They have no need to do this. They are complete in themselves. But having done this the adopted child comes to affect them. They love him and can be hurt by him. In a similar way, although God was under no internal pressure to create us, once having done so he allows us to move him. He is glad in our gladness and sad in our sorrow. We matter to him and therefore he has bestowed on us the power to affect him.

The Christian understanding of God as Holy Trinity is not a mere form of words nor is it an optional extra. It goes to the heart of the faith, indeed it *is* the faith. It has been said that it is the one doctrine the Church has. It is not so much that other views of God are untrue as that they are one sided. The Jew and the Muslim believe that God is creator/Father. He is. But God is more than this. The mystic on the Indian subcontinent believes God is within us as the centre of our being. He is. But God is more than this. Some Christians say that 'Jesus lives' and that we can have a relationship with him now. We can. But God is more than this. These are all partial views of God, which find their completeness within the Christian understanding of God as Father, Son and Holy Spirit.

Too often the doctrine of God as Holy Trinity has been treated as a form of words for speculation rather than the heart of a religion which is to be lived. Every time we pray, we can begin 'In the name of the Father and of the Son and of the Holy Spirit' (perhaps making the sign of the Cross), and then we can pause to reflect that the God to whom we pray is nothing less than that. Whenever we pray, whenever we think of God, whenever we seek to live out the Christian life, it is nothing less than the whole Trinity, Father, Son and Holy Spirit who is present with us. God is present as the creative source of all that exists, who moment by moment holds us in being. He is the Father upon whom we depend. He is the eternal Son who shares our life and stands beside us as our friend and brother. He is the Holy Spirit, God within us, our true centre, the life and love from whom we live.

The Christian understanding of God as Holy Trinity is the most sublime and glorious notion revealed to man. In it every view of God finds its focus and fulfilment, for God is not just beyond us, but beside us and within us. Every difficulty finds its resolution, for God is not just a reality outside us, to whom we can relate, but a reality into whose heart of fire we have been taken. But this understanding of God is one to be prayed and lived.

O God, Father, moment by moment you hold me in being,
on you I depend.
O God, Eternal Son, sharing my life as friend and brother,
in you I trust.
O God, Holy Spirit, life and love within me,
from you I live.
O God, you are the one I reach out to,
mystery beyond human thinking,
love beyond our comprehending.

Yet because you are love you have reached out to me,
joined me to Christ,
taken me into the very heart of your divine life,
come close to me as Father and brother.
Because you are love, you yourself have come to dwell in me.
So it is your love within me reaching out
to your love beyond me.
O God beyond me, God beside me, God within me,
Father, Son and Holy Spirit,
three persons in one God,
you are ever to be worshipped and adored.

Questions for discussion

1   If one really came to believe that, in Christ, God and man, heaven and earth, are joined never to be unjoined, how might this change one's view of life?

2   Examine any feelings you might have that the way God is normally portrayed is too small, narrow and jejune. How might a proper understanding of God as Holy Trinity enlarge and deepen our whole understanding of God?

3   How can the belief that God is Father, Son and Holy Spirit come to shape and permeate our whole approach to God, and in particular our prayers?

4   What gift (or gifts) of the Holy Spirit do you think you have been given?

4

Life Everlasting

DEATH AS AN ENEMY

For most people most of the time it is of little consequence whether or not there is a life after death. The life we now have to live is either so absorbing or so demanding we do not give the matter much consideration. But, as the next chapter on suffering makes plain, it is doubtful whether, without a belief in a worthwhile life after this one, it is possible to believe that God is a God of love. The question of whether there is an afterlife is intimately related to the question of whether there is a God.

When her mother died, Simone de Beauvoir commented that at all times and in all circumstances death was an enemy. This is a natural reaction to death by someone who loves life. A Methodist minister is his eighty second year, who loved the Lord and thought himself well prepared for death, was told he would have to have an operation which there was only a fifty per cent chance of surviving. He said he was overcome with a sense of how much he loved life and how little he wanted to die. Even if we have been only moderately lucky we will have found some things to love in life, and leaving them for ever will be a loss. If we love deeply people who are still living, the pain will be great. So death is an enemy. It deprives us of what we most cherish in our own lives and those of others. Anyone who has been bereaved and who has experienced the devastation, desolation, grief, anger, guilt and deep sadness that come with the loss of someone we love, knows only too well death in this guise.

In the Bible there is a further reason why death is regarded as an enemy. It leads, or can lead, to a final separation from God. When we do something wrong, this cuts us off from God. Death makes this separation permanent. If friends go away we may miss them a good deal, but if we have been close to them in some way they remain close. If on the other hand the person who leaves is someone with whom there have been terrible quarrels, their departure puts the seal on this estrangement. It finalises and brings home the rupture in the relationship. Because of human sin this is what death does for us in relation to God. So, as St Paul put it, 'the sting of death is sin'. (1 Corinthians 15.56.) Hence, as he also said, 'The last enemy to be destroyed is death'. (1 Corinthians 15.26.)

GROUNDS FOR BELIEF IN AN AFTER-LIFE

Some people seem to expect the resurrection of the dead as some kind of automatic pension program. But of course, we have no inherent right to a life after this one. Nor is there anything about us which automatically lives on. The Christian hope of heaven is based four square on the character of God and on that alone. This can be summed up by three statements.

First, God himself is immortal and if he so wished he could share his immortality with us.

Second, God is loving and wishes to give us his best gifts. Jesus taught that if human fathers, flawed as they are, know how to give good things to their children, how much more does our heavenly Father give good things to those who ask him.

Third, God has promised us life with him for ever. This is the unanimous view of the writers of the New Testament.

50

The same truth can be looked at from another point of view, that of our experience of God. It was Paul's experience that nothing in this life, no hardship, no suffering, could separate him from the love of God as he had come to know it in Christ. He believed that death could no more cut him off either. (Romans 8.38.) It was also his experience, and that of other Christians, that the power of God to bring life from death was present in the Christian community. There is continuity between the God who raised Jesus from the dead, the God who brings faith to birth in us now and the God who will make us new for eternity. The continuity is provided by God himself, who brings hope out of despair, love out of hate, life out of death. As we come to know this God and his transforming power we develop a trustful confidence that he can raise us from death for a life everlasting.

To those who are interested in psychic or spiritualist phenomena and other alleged evidence that the personality can survive death, these arguments in favour of such an important truth as everlasting life may seem brief and inadequate. But the contention here is that our hope of a worthwhile life beyond death is grounded in God alone. This hope can be looked at from two points of view. It is God's own life which he has promised to share with us. It is a life which we have already begun to experience in Christ (eternal life).

DEATH AS A FRIEND

For these reasons death is not just an enemy to be fought. It can become a friend to be welcomed. The lives of the saints are full of stories of death bed scenes in which the saint goes to God full of longing and radiant with joy. 'The time of my departure is at hand, and my soul longs to see Christ my king in his beauty,' wrote Bede, a statement which can stand for the millions of Christians who have died expressing similar thoughts. 'Welcome, sister death,' said St Francis.

For those who die young or tragically death is far from being a friend. This is part of the larger problem of suffering considered in the next chapter but it raises also the question of the possibility of further stages of growth after this life. So many die with lives cut short. Too many die after a lifetime of frustration and lack of fulfilment. If death is to be a friend of all there must be not only the possibility of life beyond it but a life in which all that has been stunted or nipped in the bud is enabled to grow.

RESURRECTION

Many people in our own society and others believe that we have souls that live on when we die. The word soul is important for it indicates that we are more than the sum of our individual physical parts. We can pray, recognise right and wrong, love and think creative thoughts. It is obvious that there is some relationship between our mental activity and the electrical and chemical processes that go on in the brain. Certain operations on the brain can change our character, drugs can alter our mood. But this does not mean that our mental activity will cease to function with the death of our brains. Some scientists have argued that mind is in fact prior to, and independent of, the brain, which acts as a kind of focus or transmitter of mental activity. Though there is a correspondence between what goes on in the mind and what goes on in the brain, the former may be only temporally dependent on the latter. Whatever the truth of this matter, the Christian faith bases its belief in life everlasting not on anything inherently immortal about us, but upon God's revealed character as one who loves us and wants to give us all we can take from him. Corresponding to this is the belief in 'the resurrection of the body'. This is not a literal statement that our physical bodies are going to be resuscitated. It is a symbolic statement preserving four essential truths.

First, who we really are is a mystery. Our bodies change every seven years. And which is the real me? The person I was at 20, or 30 or 70? All we can say is that the essential person we are, the thinking, choosing, loving, praying self that has developed in the course of so many experiences is in the last analysis known to God alone. We could put it like this. Even if it is true that when I die and my knowledge of things ceases, God's knowledge of me does not cease. I have been known to God (better than I know myself) and I continue to be known to him. I have a continuing existence in his mind.

Second, this true self will be as it were 'reclothed' with a medium of expression appropriate to an eternal existence. If our existence in heaven is going to be as real as it is now we need to be more than an idea. We need to be a particular existence with a means of expressing ourselves and recognising others doing the same. We need, in short, to have something corresponding to a body. In this life we communicate in different ways, through speech, writing, drawing and movement for example. After death there will be another more glorious way of expressing ourselves. A composer with a line of music in his head puts it down on paper in notation marks. Later a conductor and orchestra interpret those marks and turn them into music that is heard. St. Paul says that 'it is raised a spiritual body'. (1 Corinthians 15.44.) We do not know what this spiritual body will be like; all we can say is what St. Paul said, that there will be both continuity and discontinuity with the personalities we know now.

Third, whatever it is that God has in store for us, it is

sheer gift. There is a Christian suspicion of the whole idea of the immortality of the soul because of its suggestion that we have an automatic claim on what lies ahead. But we do not. This life is a gift. The one that comes next is also gift. The assertion in the Creed, 'We believe . . . in the resurrection of the body,' safeguards this truth. In death we are reduced to nothing. Death is an enemy taking away everything that is most precious to us, finalising our estrangement from God. But God in his mercy creates us anew for eternal life. All is grace, sheer grace.

Fourth, belief in the resurrection also safeguards the truth that in heaven we will be more, not less, than the selves we now are. We will not just be shadowy whisps of what we once were. We will be more fully and richly ourselves than ever before, capable of recognising and being recognised by others. The sceptic within us finds this impossible to envisage. But belief that heaven is more sublime than anything we can imagine is inherent in the whole New Testament.

JUDGEMENT

Anyone who has been in a court of law knows that the thought of being judged by anyone — let alone Almighty God — is an unnerving one. It would be nice to do away with the idea of divine judgement altogether. But can we? Sometimes when we meet a person of outstanding qualities this leads us to question ourselves. Their depth makes us feel shallow; their authenticity makes us feel a fraud; their integrity makes us feel cheap. The other person does not intend to have that effect on us. They greet us with the utmost warmth and friendliness. But. being the kind of person they are, we cannot help but become aware of the contrast with ourselves.

It is a common experience that, when someone dies,

those close to them suffer from feelings of guilt and remorse. We regret harsh words spoken, realise there was more we could have done. Pastorally of course people need to be listened to and then reassured when they feel like this, as we all do. But these very rare moods of self-questioning sometimes express truth. A man who lost his estranged wife and two children in a car crash blamed himself bitterly for giving them a car. Of course he was not to blame for that. Then he let out a revealing remark, 'What she really wanted was me.' Something inside him recognised that his financial generosity to his ex-wife was a compensation for refusing to give her what she really wanted. Such moments of insight suggest that the idea of judgement cannot be eliminated as easily as we would like.

What we can and must get rid of is the idea, which too many people still carry round with them, of God as a hanging judge, a Judge Jeffries writ large. God is not like that at all. He is like Jesus going out of his way to sit at table with sinners. He is like the father in the parable of the prodigal son who saw his son at a distance and ran to embrace him. God does not reject us. On the contrary he ceaselessly goes out to us to press us close to himself. But we cannot know his great love for us without at the same time knowing ourselves as we really are. The more intensely we know God's love for us the more painfully aware we are of our own lack of love.

The subject of judgement seems gloomy, but for the Christian there are two crucial facts which light up the subject with joy. First it is God in Christ who is the judge, the only judge there is. Second, Christians have been welcomed, accepted, forgiven by him already. St Paul talks about this using the imagery of the law court. 'We have been justified by grace through faith.' St John talks about it using the imagery of light. The light of Christ has come into the world, revealing things for what they are. Evil is shown up and flees from him. Those who are of the light have responded to him. For John there is a significant sense in which the divine judgement has taken place already.

To put it quite simply we are, through Christ, already at one with, in a right relationship with, God. The Christian believes that nothing will sever this union, for God's love never ceases.

HELL

God does not send anyone to hell but the possibility of hell always exists. We cannot believe that man is free to respond to goodness and God, without at the same time accepting that some people might refuse to respond to goodness and God for ever. Modern literature has a number of convincing pictures of hell. Sartre's play *Huis Clos* depicts four people locked up in a small room with a single bare light for ever. They are in a permanent state of recrimination, self-justification and antagonism, hence the famous line, 'Hell is other people'. In Samuel Beckett's play *Play* three people live their relationship with one another over and over again. There is a deliberate ambiguity about where this takes place. It is either just this side of death or just the other side. In either case it is hell.

We cannot believe man is free without at the same time believing in the possibility of hell. But God does not send people to hell. He ceaselessly reaches out to draw us to himself. Moreover, he has all eternity to work in. If we lock ourselves up in ourselves the light of his love plays upon us endlessly. If we turn our backs on sheer goodness, sheer goodness waits with hands s:retched out; waits for ever. If we shrink back into the dungeon we have made for ourselves God keeps throwing us the key to let ourselves out. So, in the light of this, can we believe that even one single soul will finally languish for ever in hell? We can hope, we can trust, that God's boundless, endless love will finally win all hatred over to himself.

PURGATORY

Martin Luther and the other sixteenth century reformers firmly rejected the idea of purgatory. This was because the view of purgatory then held, at least by the popular mind, was un-Christian. People thought that heaven was something we had to merit by our efforts and that, through the right prayers and good works, we could, as it were, earn our passage there. This view strikes at the very heart of the Christian faith, for the good news is that we are already 'accepted in the beloved'. The Christian life is not an attempt to earn heaven but a response to God's love for us, as it has been shown in Christ. Heaven (or eternal life, as St John calls it) is already ours. No effort on our part can make us at one with God. But God has made us at one with himself by forgiving us and making us a limb in Christ's body.

In so far as purgatory implies that we can make ourselves right with God through our efforts it must be rejected. God has already acted to put us in a right relationship with himself. But this does not mean that the concept of purgatory must be totally rejected. St Paul says that all that we do will be tested as though by fire. 'If any man's work is burned up, he will suffer loss, though he himself will be saved, but only as through fire.' (1 Cor. 3.15.) In other words, as we draw closer to God's love that love will not only warm and thrill us but it will burn away all that is not built on the foundation of Christ. This coming into the nearer presence of God after death and the consequent purification it brings may, if we think in terms of time, be instantaneous. But there may be something about it corresponding to different stages. Hindus and some Buddhists believe in reincarnation. They think that we live our lives on this earth over and over again until full spiritual development has taken place, when we are released from the cycle of death and rebirth. Christians don't believe this, for various reasons. But the idea of further growth, through different stages, may be an important aspect of the truth. These stages, if they exist, are not on this earth but in other dimensions of existence.

Some people think that talk of further stages of growth after this life takes away from the moral seriousness of the choices we make now. The Bible suggests that there is an urgency about how we order our present existence. There is an urgency. But it is not lessened by the prospect of further stages of development in the hereafter.

The reason we have only a limited life span and do not live for ever on this earth seems to be connected with the need to have a definite horizon. Most of us can plan what we want to do during a day, a week, a year perhaps. Beyond that it gets difficult, though as we get older we can suggest certain broad goals we would like to attain during a lifetime. If we had the prospect of living for ever on earth it would be difficult for anything to have a shape. There would always be the very reasonable thought: 'Well, I won't study music now, or gardening or whatever, I can always do that in a thousand years or so.' The fact that we have only a limited period of time means that we have to develop a sense of priorities − we cannot do everything in one lifetime − and this in turn means we define ourselves as a particular person. For it is through deciding what to do with our life, our time, money, energy, that we shape ourselves. So the fact that we have only a short life span is important. It gives just the right sense of urgency to our decisions. We cannot prevaricate for ever. That, no doubt, is why God in his wisdom has made it this way and why death is a kind of curtain across the future. For we have no clear picture of what lies beyond. What we have is a sure hope based upon what God has revealed of his purpose for us in Christ. Enough to go on but not a map. Talk of 'further stages of growth' does not take away from the reality and seriousness of choice in this life. We still plan for this week, even though we are likely to be alive for the week following as well. We still have to decide what to do with our life, even if there is a reasonable prospect of further development after death.

HEAVEN

People sometimes think that the prospect of heaven is mercenary. We have been taught to do our duty without expecting any reward. If we do just that, isn't it the highest kind of life we can aim for? To the morally minded atheist the idea of heaven can seem almost trivial. But we have to distinguish two different kinds of reward, extrinsic and intrinsic. When the reward is extrinsic, as with a knighthood, there is no essential connection between the reward and the activity for which it was given. A person who has helped overseas exports might just as well have been made a peer, given a CBE or any other honour. In the case of an intrinsic reward just the opposite is true. There is an integral connection between the reward and the activity. A couple who are courting and saving for marriage eventually achieve their aim. During their long engagement they look forward to the time when they can live together as man and wife in their own home. What they look forward to is where their love leads. It is the natural outcome of their feelings for one another. There is nothing arbitrary about it. In the same way heaven is where the Christian's relationship with God leads. It is not like a decoration pinned on the chest. It is the natural or rather supernatural outcome of all his faith and hope and love as a Christian. People who are engaged can at the same time appreciate the one they love and look forward to the time when they are married. In the same way a Christian can rejoice in his present relationship with God and look for its consummation in heaven.

Heaven is of course impossible to imagine. All we can say is that the most fulfilling and blessed moments of our lives now are but faint reflections of what one day will be. Do we appreciate beauty in nature or art? God is, as St. Augustine put it, 'beauty most ancient and withal so fresh'. Have we experienced moments of genuine love? God himself is love beyond compare and the source of all love. Have we, in the family, or·with friends, or in a community, experienced something of true fellowship with other people? It is a taste, however weak, of heaven. Have we had moments of genuine prayer? Heaven means an unbroken communion with God. Have we been lifted out of ourselves in worship? Heaven is where our desire to recognise and respond to what is of worth finds all it needs. There we will be transfixed by perfect beauty, truth and goodness.

THE COMMUNION OF SAINTS

The Christian life is not a solitary life either here or in the hereafter. To be a Christian is to be with an innumerable body of believers, both those on earth and those who 'rejoice with us but upon another shore and in a greater light'. The great goal of God in creation is the communion of saints, a community of persons bonded and bound together in the love of God. The communion of saints is the crown and climax of the whole evolutionary process. First matter, then life, then life that thinks and knows that it thinks, then

Christ. Finally all things and people incorporate in Christ, when God will be all in all.

For the Buddhist, becoming part of the 'all' means the obliteration of the individual personality. But, as was suggested in chapter three in the discussion on the Triity, unity and individuality, far from excluding one another, in fact mutually reinforce each other. Both in relationships with other human beings and in our relationship with God we discover how the closeness of love brings individuality to flower. For the Christian, becoming part of the 'all' (which is God in Christ) means that the personality is enhanced and becomes more distinctively itself.

The saints and the faithful departed are closer to us than we know. For where are those who respond to God's gracious invitation? With God himself. And where is God? With us, closer to us than we are to ourselves. There is no need for any attempt to contact the dead. All we need to do is to try to be close to God in love and prayer. Those we love are with God and God is with us.

This means that the saints can pray for us and we can pray for the departed. The saints, because they are closer to God now than when they were on earth, share even more intimately in his work. Part of that work is interceding for people according to Christ's will. We can, if we want, ask for the prayers of the saints in general or one saint in particular. We have friends on earth and sometimes we ask one of them to pray for us. We also have friends in heaven and it is just as natural to ask them to pray for us. It no more takes away from the centrality of Christ and his grace than asking an earthly friend to pray for us. All prayer, whether on earth or in heaven, is Christ praying in and through us.

It is just as natural to pray for the departed. More often than now happens, our prayers should express thanks. We should remember with gratitude particular aspects of the life and character of someone we have loved and give thanks to God for them. But this prayer can also include the request that the loved one be drawn ever deeper into God. The traditional words, 'Rest eternal grant unto them O Lord. Let light perpetual shine upon them', have a never fading truth and beauty. Praying for the departed should in no way be associated with the idea of purgatory rejected by the reformers. The departed person can come to God only in so far as they recognise and respond to God's love shown forth in Christ. But God works through our prayers both for the living and the departed.

THE CHRISTIAN APPROACH TO DEATH AND ETERNAL LIFE

From what has been said it is possible to sum up the Christian attitude to death and everlasting life in five points.

First, he will be honest about his own fear and reluctance to die — if that is what his feelings are. Christ prayed in Gethsemane 'Father, take this cup from me.' If the person is with others in a similar position he will try to help them articulate their fears and anxieties.

Second, he will have an attitude of trust. Death from our point of view means entering a darkness, an apparent annihilation. But God is with us in the darkness. He will lead us through and make us anew for eternity. 'Though I go through the valley of the shadow of death thy rod and staff comfort me still.' Death, like sleep, means a letting go into the dark unknown. On the cross Jesus said the prayer that Jewish mothers taught their children to say as they went to sleep. 'Father, into thy hands I commit my spirit.'

Third, the Christian dies in hope. It is difficult to imagine the exact form in which this hope will find its fulfilment. But it is a hope grounded in the thought of the collect, 'O God, who hast prepared for them that love thee such good things as pass man's understanding.'

Fourth, this hope is not an optional extra. It is one of the essential pillars of the Christian faith. It is true that the people of the Old Testament believed in God for a long time before coming to believe in a life after death. This was also the experience of C. S. Lewis. He believed in God whilst at the same time being hostile to the whole idea of the afterlife. But once one has grasped the depth of God's love for us it is difficult to see how it can fail to include the prospect of life with him in the communion of saints.

Fifth, the prospect of eternity does not distract one from this world and its value but enhances the significance of what we are doing now. Marx, Freud and a host of lesser mortals have criticised the Christian hope of a hereafter for taking people's minds off their proper concerns in this world. It may be true that the Church in particular periods has been guilty of concentrating too much on what will come after death, to the neglect of what ought to be done to change things for the better now. Certainly whilst we are on earth our major concern must be with God's will in relation to the things of the earth. As Winston Churchill once put it: 'There may very well be two worlds but I prefer to take them one at a time.' The Christian wants to say something stronger than this. There *are* two worlds and, whilst we should take them one at a time, the fact that we have been made for eternity, and not just the all too brief seventy years, casts its bright light on all we think or do.

Questions for discussion

1   Do you agree with the point of view of this chapter, that our hope of a worthwhile life after this one is based upon God and upon him alone?

2   How, if at all, is it possible to convey something of the Christian hope to those who are deeply grieving?

3   When you remember those you have known and loved, who are now dead, do you find it possible to remember them in prayer before God? If so, what kind of prayers seem natural to you?

4   How can the communion of saints become a more central part of Christian living?

5

Suffering and a God of Love

It was suggested in chapter one that faith in God is natural to human beings. The main problem for belief is not trying to prove God's existence (which by the nature of the case can be neither proved nor disproved) but the presence of so much suffering in the world. People have, as it were, an initial bias towards faith in a loving and wise power behind the universe, but reflection on life's miseries soon leads them to question and perhaps even to deny that faith. It's not the existence of suffering as such which poses the problem. Most people can shrug off a certain amount of frustration and hardship. It's the intensity and extent of suffering that calls belief in a loving God into question. A woman had rodent cancer. Over a period of twenty years this made a larger and larger hole in her face. She became unable to eat, talk or smell properly. She looked so grotesque that she could not go out. At one time she came into contact with a fringe Christian group who claimed that if she only prayed enough or in the right way she would get better. She did not get better, and so she was left with yet another burden to bear. This is an extreme example of suffering. But often it is the less dramatic examples that pose the question most poignantly, such as people who are totally frustrated both in their work and their personal life. They get no satisfaction from their job and they have no fulfilling relationships. They suffer from minor physical ailments and recurring depression. What, in the end, does the life of such a person add up to? The argument against the existence of a loving God (and the moral passion that often goes with it) needs to be taken with the utmost seriousness. [1] 'Dark, unfeeling, and unloving powers determine human destiny,' wrote Freud, a view shared for some of his life by Thomas Hardy.

FREE TO CHOOSE

Much human suffering is caused by the deliberate ill will of other human beings or their uncaring negligence. The amount of suffering attributable to this cause is more than might at first be apparent. Something like 600 million people in the world are suffering from malnutrition. There is in fact enough food to go round. But it is distributed unfairly and priorities are wrong. A high percentage of almost every national budget in the world goes on arms. Money which could be used to feed the starving and overcome disease is spent on weapons designed to kill other people. This statement is not made in a simplistic way. But the fact is that we are caught up in a network of relationships in which there have been a million, million wrong choices, each one arising out of, and perpetuating a flawed system.

Some philosophers have suggested that we are not free to choose other than what we do choose. But this is highly unlikely. If everything was determined it would make any rational agreement or disagreement impossible. For what each person said would simply be the inevitable outcome of whatever chemical processes were operating in their mind and body at the time. Even the statement 'Everything is determined' would be determined, which is a reduction to absurdity.

1. I have tried to do this in 'True Unbelief' in *Stewards of the Mysteries of God* ed. Eric James, DLT 1979.

Furthermore, if everything was determined, consciousness would have no function, which, given what we know about the nature of evolution, would be very strange. In fact, consciousness does have a function. As one psychiatrist put it, 'consciousness transmutes instinctual drives in such a way that the outcome of any act of decision is *not* solely determined by the relative strength of the instinctual forces involved.'

To say that we are free to choose does not mean that our decisions are arbitrary. They arise out of the person we are. Moreover, the extent of our real freedom is probably more limited than most people realise. We are each of us the product of a particular genetic endowment and formative experiences in early childhood. We are always in a social setting which exerts pressures to behave in certain ways rather than others. Our area of manoeuvre is extremely limited. But we do have some freedom and this is crucial. For God has endowed us with something of his own godlike quality. We can think and choose, and come to love and pray. God has chosen to make not puppets or robots but free beings, capable of making creative decisions, able to further goodness or wreak havoc.

If it is God's purpose to create free beings he cannot, on the one hand give us rational minds and wills of our own and then block every decision we make. Parents learn that they have to give their children more freedom as they get older. Often this process is painful for both sides, and parents are highly conscious of the risk they are taking from the moment they let their children cycle to school to the time they let them go out to their first late party. But parents don't want automatons, and no more does God. So he gives us enough rope both to hang others and ourselves, if that is what we insist on doing.

Much suffering in the world is caused by wrong human choices. God allows this suffering to occur because it is his purpose to create beings like himself, free to choose. But a great deal of suffering is not attributable to human choice − many diseases, floods, earthquakes, and droughts, for example. Three points can be made. First, to exist is to exist with a life of one's own. We are familiar with this as it applies to ourselves. But it applies to everything from an electron to a star. 'Running oneself one's own way is the same thing as existing', as Austin Farrer put it. 'If God had made things to exist but not to run their own way, he would have made them to exist, and not to exist.' In other words, not just ourselves, but everything that exists has a real independence and this is implicit in the very idea of creation.

Second, what we think of as natural disasters are only such if they affect sentient life in a painful way. There is, for example, nothing wrong with an earthquake per se. Earthquakes occur because the inside of the earth is still hot whereas the surface is a crust. This is the condition that has produced life. If the earth was still molten, life would not exist. If, on the other hand, the earth had cooled down so much that it had become cold and solid, life would have died out. There may be other forms of life on other planets or in worlds unknown, but life as we know it has been produced on a planet which has cooled enough to produce a crust but not so much that it has gone solid. But the conditions which enable life to be produced are also the conditions which still allow a certain amount of movement of the earth's crust. The earthquakes and volcanoes so produced are not evil in themselves. They are the product of natural forces blinding away at being themselves.

Third, given God's overall purpose of creating free beings, there is a limit to the extent of his 'intervention' in the processes of nature. In order for our minds to develop we need a stable environment. If the world in which we lived became unpredictable, minds could not emerge and God's purpose would be frustrated. When children first go to school they need continuity between what they learn one day and the next. If on the first day they were taught that this sign A was pronounced aaaa, and on the next day they were taught that it was pronounced mmmm, and on the third day they were told that the same sign was pronounced peeee, the children would never learn the alphabet or how to read. In order to learn we need to build on previous experience. Exactly the same is true in the wider world. On the assumption that there is continuity between one day and the next we make predictions on the basis of which we live and learn to think. Imagine an Alice in Wonderland kind of world. Someone is about to drown, so water is turned to ice to stop them sinking — but what about people nearby who are in the process of drinking that same water? Someone is about to fall down some steps and the laws of gravity are reversed to hold her in mid-air. But what about the people who are walking down the steps normally? They suddenly find that they cannot move. Someone is about to run over a child and the car stops short in a miraculously short space. But what about the car behind? Unless another miracle is performed it will run straight into the car that has stopped short in an unpredictably short distance. And if a miracle took place a second time what about the car behind that and so on? A world in which God continually intervened to reverse the laws of nature would become so chaotic that mind as we know it would not survive. So, a certain stability, regularity and continuity in nature, with the corresponding risk of accident, is an essential condition for the bringing to birth of rational souls. Talk about 'laws of nature' can imply something impersonal and cold. But what is the regularity in nature but a reflection of God's faithfulness? Whenever the sun rises or an apple falls, the grass grows, or a kettle boils, God is revealing some tiny glimpse of his faithfulness. Therefore this emphasis on the necessity of stability and continuity in our environment is not just a philosophical point. To the eye of faith, the order in nature is a sign of the God who can be trusted.

It is possible for us to understand how God, once having given us freedom, leaves us free to make mistakes. Further, we can see how, given his purpose of creating free beings, it is necessary for us to have an environment which is predictable. But a question still remains. Why should God have created us as part of a material world? We could perhaps have been made like the angels instead of sentient beings in a world where the possibility of accident is so high. The most ingenious answer to this question was suggested by Austin Farrer and taken up by John Hick. If we had been created in the immediate presence of God we would have no real freedom. Created fully good, in a totally good environment, we would be completely captivated by the divine goodness. We would have no more freedom than a shaving of metal before a powerful magnet. So in order to give us real freedom God creates us at a distance from himself. Not indeed a physical distance, for that would be impossible. God is the ground of our being, closer to us than we are ourselves. But there is a kind of distance of knowing, a screen, between us and God. This screen is the material world. It ensures that we have no overwhelming knowledge of God and that we can come to know him only in so far as we want to do so.

There is a further consideration adding to the force of this argument. When we are born we have, like all members of the animal world, a strong desire to preserve ourselves in existence. If we didn't have this we would quickly perish both as individuals and a species. This means that not only are we born into a world which provides a kind of screen between ourselves and God but we are born with a strong desire to look after our own interests. In order to know God at all not only do we have to desire to do so but we have to transend the innate selfishness that is in all of us. God is not totally hidden. Something of himself is revealed through everything he has made and a young child can, from the first dawning of consciousness, come into a true relationship with God, but this relationship is never forced upon us. We grow in knowledge of God only in so far as we seek God and in so far as we can look away from ourselves and our own concerns to God and his purpose for us. 'Blessed are the pure in heart for they shall see God.'

WHAT GOD DOES ABOUT SUFFERING

God has given us and the whole natural order a real independence. He has created this order and made us belong to it, as part of his purpose of bringing into being creatures who are genuinely free. But God does not just wind up the universe like a clock and then let it tick away. He shares its life at every point. Most human beings have some capacity for sympathy, a word made up of two Greek words meaning to suffer with. We can enter into the situation of other people and to some extent feel what they feel, see life through their eyes. God's capacity to enter into our minds and hearts is unlimited. It is not limited by any physical considerations. He is not cut off from our spirits as we are cut off from other people by a wall of flesh and blood. The divine spirit has direct access to the human spirit. But, just as important, his love is in no way

71

limited. He has a boundless capacity for transcending his own life and entering into ours. He feels what we feel more intensely than we do ourselves, for his love for us is greater than our love for ourselves.

God is not a detached spectator of the universe. His love enters into every human life sharing its joy and woe. Of this the incarnation is the great sign and pledge. In Christ, God knows the precariousness and vulnerability of human life. On the cross he experiences the extreme limit of alienation and darkness. When Studdert Kennedy, the first World War padre, nicknamed 'Woodbine Willie' from his habit of distributing woodbines wherever he went, was visiting in a hospital one of the badly wounded soldiers asked him what God was like. Studdert Kennedy simply held out his crucifix. God bears our human sorrow within himself.

God is, in the philosopher Whitehead's words, the fellow sufferer who understands. But he is more than this. In Christ he not only enters into our human situation, he overcomes all that is contrary to divine love. Through the cross and resurrection a decisive victory has been achieved. In chapter two it was pointed out how Christ died on the cross the death of a cursed blasphemer. He died the death of one totally alienated from God. There are many forms of suffering that Christ did not have to undergo. But if 'all that matters is to be at one with the living God', there is no evil worse than this. Then Christ was raised from the dead. His resurrection reveals sin to be overcome, suffering transfigured and death defeated. Furthermore it means that in Christ, fully God and fully man, there is a unity between heaven and earth which can never be destroyed. When we face the worst situations known to us, populations bombed to death in war, torture, disease of mind and body; even the extreme, beyond words, horror of millions of Jews being exterminated in concentration camps, we can see them in the light of the death and resurrection of Christ. As a result of him, and through the incorporation of humanity into his life, we have a hope that the worst imaginable evils will be overcome, the most excruciating pain of mind and body transfigured, the most humiliating death redeemed.

The death and resurrection of Christ were regarded by the first Christians as the beginning of the end of the world. And so they are. They are a sign and pledge of what will ultimately be, God all in all. God's purposes go beyond this mortal life and find their fulfilment in a community of love beyond space and time. It is no good pretending that Christians can discuss the challenge of suffering to God's love without bringing in the death and resurrection of Christ and God's promise of heaven. So many die young, so many die frustrated of any chance of personal or spiritual growth. If this life is the only one there is, either we would have to say that there is no God of love, or that the purpose of this love could be finally frustrated.

The Christian faith is all of a piece. There are a number of central pillars so placed that, if one is taken away, the whole edifice falls to the ground. This is why the problem posed by suffering has been left to this point. It cannot be properly considered until the essentials of Christian faith have been sketched out. Only in the light of all these essentials can some kind of answer be made. From the point of view of meeting the challenge posed by suffering the three essentials are:

First, God has given both us and the whole natural order a real independence and freedom.

Second, in Christ God himself enters into the worst experience that human life can batter us with, the experience of total darkness and alienation.

Third, God's purpose of love will finally prevail. In the end, 'All will be well and all manner of thing will be well'. Of this the cross and the resurrection is the sign and promise. There is a unity between God and man which nothing, not even death itself, can finally destroy.

BUT IS IT WORTH IT?

Life is hard, very hard. Even when the above considerations have been adduced it is still understandable if someone says, 'But is it all worth it?' The most famous form of this argument is that by Ivan Karamazov. After telling various stories about the death of children he says: 'Tell me frankly, I appeal to you — answer me: imagine that it is you yourself who are erecting the edifice of human destiny with the aim of making men happy in the end, of giving them peace and contentment at last, but that to do that it is absolutely necessary, and indeed quite inevitable, to torture to death only one tiny creature, the little girl who beat her breast with her little fist, and to found the edifice on her unavenged tears — would you consent to be the architect on those conditions? Tell me and do not lie.' Ivan believes in God. He even believes in heaven. But the presence of so much innocent suffering in the world forces him to the conclusion that God was not justified in taking the risk of creation. 'It is not God that I do not accept, Alyosha. I merely most respectfully return him the ticket.'

Whether or not God was justified in taking the risk of creation depends on every creature he has made saying that they are glad they lived. If at the end of the whole creative process, in that transtemporal, transpatial community of the blessed, every creature who has ever lived blesses God for their existence it will have been worth it. God will have been justified. Second, the question about whether or not the experience of living is worthwhile can only be answered by each individual for himself. It is not a question we can answer for anyone else or which anyone else can answer for us. Sometimes we can look at a person, suffering, say, from paralysis, and wonder how on earth they can want to go on living. We think to ourselves that if were were in that position, we would wish ourselves dead. But so often that person does not feel like that. They have found joys and a fulfilment that we are not fully capable of appreciating. Whether life is worthwhile is a question that each person has to answer for himself.

As humans we experience a mixture of good fortune and bad. We have enjoyable times and miserable ones. But very often it seems that, when something comes good for us, the painful past fades away. Two lovers have been separated for a long time and this has led to misunderstanding and tension. But, when they meet, their happiness in each other's presence makes all this drop away. An athlete has many years of struggle and hardship. Many times he wonders if it is worth it. He has setbacks and times of depression. He sees himself missing out on many experiences that are worthwhile. But in the end, as he stands on the rostrum to receive his gold, all this is forgotten. The thrill of the present moment throws a new light over everything. Heaven is an environment of total joy. In the presence of God all the anguish that has gone before fades into insignificance. It is not quite forgotten. Wounds remain in the body of the risen Christ. But the injuries have been transfigured. The wounds are healed or healing. There will be no pain that will not be seen in a new light and transformed when we come into the sun of God's love.

This is the Christian hope. In deep misery this hope does not always seem very real; nevertheless, even when things are at their worst, we seem to have some almost instinctive sense that things may not be so bad as they seem. The capacity of ordinary people to struggle on with courage and often with gusto, is an ever recurring witness to the worthwhileness of the human endeavour despite all the hardships. Camus once said that the main problem in human life was suicide. We might put it somewhat differently and ask why it is that the vast majority of human beings do not commit suicide.

In D. H. Lawrence's novel *Sons and Lovers*, Paul Morel's mother says to him that she wants him to be happy. 'Battle — battle — battle — and suffer. It's about all you do, as far as I can see,' she says. Paul replies that this is the best; but again Mrs Morel says, 'One ought to be happy, one ought.' 'Never mind, Little,' he replies, 'So long as you don't feel life's a paltry and a miserable business, the rest doesn't matter, happiness or unhappiness.' She presses Paul to her and says, 'But I want you to be happy.' 'Eh, my dear,' says Paul, 'Say rather you want me to live.' In this dialogue we get the clear sense, shared by so many people, that struggling to live with courage and integrity is what matters most. Life is more than a question of balancing pleasant experiences with unpleasant. This is why, despite so much that is ghastly and threatening to the future, people go on having children. The belief that the experience of living is worthwhile and that God was justified in creating beings capable of knowing anguish as well as joy, is based not only on a hope that in the end all suffering will be transfigured but on our present intuition that there is something more involved than happiness or unhappiness.

THE PRACTICAL IMPLICATIONS

From these considerations certain practical conclusions can be drawn. First, wherever it is possible to reduce or eliminate suffering, we should do so. Christ healed the sick and cast out demons. In his ministry, the age old longing for a renewal of human life began to be fulfilled. What Christ did has been the inspiration for millions of attempts to alleviate suffering, from the founding of the great hospitals and orphanages to works of individual charity.

Second, we have to make a distinction between what God directly wills and what he allows. If a teenager borrows the family car and has a smash, this is not something the parents willed, but they allowed it in the sense that they gave their growing child freedom. When faced with a tragic situation, it is best to say straight out that this is not something directly willed by God. The sincere faith of some Christians leads them, mistakenly, to try to see some meaning in a tragic situation, as though God had brought it about for a particular purpose. But the dimension of tragedy cannot be eliminated from human life and it is best to admit that, whatever God might allow, certain situations are directly contrary to his prime purpose.

Third, whatever the situation, God is ceaselessly at work trying to draw some unique good out of the suffering and tragedy. Here we have to be careful. God did not design the tragedy in order for us to draw some good from it. If we had a friend who broke our leg to see how we would react or who continually shouted at us in order that we might grow in patience, we would not think much of him. We take it for granted that a friend desires our well being. So does God. What our friend wants for us, our well being, our personal fulfilment and growth, the development of all our human potential, God wants for us even more so. We can say what Keats said, that this life is a vale of soul-making, and we can draw the conclusion from this that it is necessary for us to have an environment which challenges us. If we lived under a warm sun, by a blue sea, with countless servants to do our every bidding, with nothing to stretch our body except a gentle slide into the sea and nothing to stretch our mind but a picture magazine — and all this for our whole existence (it may be very nice and necessary for a short period) — we would not develop any of the qualities we most admire in human beings. Indeed it would be doubtful if we would develop as persons at all. It is essential that life should not be too easy for us. But this is very different from saying that certain extreme situations of distress, mental breakdown for example, automatically bring about worthwhile qualities, or that they were designed with that end in view.

The fact remains, however, that human beings do sometimes reveal the most remarkable qualities as a result of suffering, and such experiences can change our whole attitude. A lady once wrote to me to say that she had a very painful cancer. This had forced her to stop doing certain things which she found enjoyable and fulfilling. She did not believe God had brought this suffering upon her. She did not like the suffering. Nevertheless, as she wrote, 'During the last two years I have begun to learn for the first time what it means to thank and praise God "at all times and in all places".' The suffering remained suffering, it did not diminish; nevertheless 'the thanking' that had come to co-exist with the suffering had led her to question whether we really knew what was meant by terms like personal growth and well being. So, as she ended, 'For me, not the pain, nor the curtailment of activity, but the meaning of "well-being", and of "personal growth" have changed; and I would not have things otherwise.'

Fourth, the Christian is not concerned with a purely intellectual answer to the question of God and suffering. He has a hope that, in the end, everything now seized with anguish will be released and glorious, but this hope leads him to practical activity. On Karl

Marx's grave appear the words, 'Philosophers have only interpreted the word, the point is however to change it.' Christianity, like Marxism is concerned with action and not words alone. The answer to 'the problem of suffering' is not a philosophy but a transformed human existence, the communion of saints, in which all potential will find its fulfilment. The task of Christians is so to open themselves to God that he may work in and through them to bring this state about. God is ceaselessly at work eliminating or reducing suffering where this can be done, and bringing some good thing from it where it cannot. Christians try to discern what God is doing in a particular situation and co-operate with him.

Questions for discussion

1 Analyse the experience of suffering of yourself or those you know. In what ways has it been destructive and diminishing? In what ways, if any, has it been productive of good?

2 Reflect on those you know who have the capacity to endure. What are the springs of their courage?

3 Is it possible to believe in a God of love without believing in Jesus as the Son of God?

4 What ills do you see being eliminated in the next fifty years?

6

The Lord's Good Pleasure

WHY SHOULD WE SEEK THE WILL OF GOD?

If a mother orders her eighteen year old daughter to help with the washing up, the daughter has, after all the pleading and arguing is over, two courses open to her. She can obey or she can refuse. If she refuses to obey her mother's order she might take a further step. She could leave home and live as though she had no parents, on the principle 'I'll do what I choose from now on'. Sadly, too many people think of the relationship between God and the world only in terms of command and obedience. The result is that some people choose disobedience and try to live life on the assumption that there is no God and that they are beholden to no one.

In another household the daughter comes in and offers to do the washing up. 'Shall I do the washing up for you, Mum?' If you asked the daughter why she was willing to help, she would probably be too reticent to answer, but it would include two factors. First, a sense of gratitude, and awareness that her mother had cared for her and looked after her for many years. Second a desire to make her mother happy, to give her a bit of a rest, to please her. In this family doing the washing up is not obedience to a command but a response to love. The same is true of the Christian life. Trying to live as a Christian is a response to God's love. God is not a regimental sergeant major writ large, and the world is not his parade ground. Jesus reveals a God who loves us. The first five chapters have sketched out the fundamentals of Christian belief. They have shown what is meant when we say God is love. We do not know that God is a God of love simply by reflecting on the world around us (which is a mixture of beauty and cruelty), nor by trusting our own feelings. We know God is a God of love through what he has revealed of himself in Jesus, in particular his death and resurrection. The Christian life is a response to this. When St Paul comes to the end of his great theological themes in his letter to the Romans he deals with the ethical implications of his beliefs. The link between the theory and the practice is provided by the words, 'I appeal to you therefore, brethren, by the mercies of God, to present your bodies as a living sacrifice, holy and acceptable to God, which is your spiritual worship.' (Romans 12.1.) Elsewhere, when urging generosity, he reminds his readers, 'For you know the grace of our Lord Jesus Christ, that though he was rich, yet for your sake he became poor, so that by his poverty you might become rich.' (2 Cor. 8.9.) Again, urging humility, he points people to what they believe. Christ, who had everything, became nothing. The only appropriate response to the sublime humility of God is humility on our part. (Phil. 2. 1-10.)

These examples from St Paul bring out the distinctive nature of the Christian life. When Malcolm Muggeridge was about to make a film of the work of Mother Teresa of Calcutta, she wrote him a letter with the words, 'Now let us do something beautiful for God'. We catch a glimpse of the beauty of God's goodness, a hint of the one whom St Augustine described as 'beauty most ancient and withall so fresh', and we choose to respond with the best we have. There is, then, only one valid reason for being a Christian. *We want to be one.* This wanting is not a matter of superficial feeling. It is a wanting with the deepest, most central part of our being. For we recognise God to be the source of all that is good and true and beautiful. We see, in what he has shown us of himself in Christ, our good, our supreme good, our sole good. In return we freely offer all that we are.

The Christian life arises out of our sense of gratitude to God and it leads to a desire to please him. We seek to know his will for us, his good pleasure. It is at this point and only at this point that the truth behind the idea of 'God's commands' comes into its own. For we cannot know anyone without at the same time knowing what they want of us, and what they want of us will be intimately linked to the kind of person they are. People who spend all their leisure time in a pub will probably ask little more of their children than that they become good drinking companions. People who are highly musical will want their children to develop any musical potential that they have within them. Parents realise that they must give their growing children freedom to carve out their own destinies, but this does not stop them from wanting, and rightly wanting, their children to grow into certain kinds of people rather than others. Because they care, they do not want their children to become drug addicts. Because they care, they want any talents they have developed. Sometimes of course parents can be oppressive in the expectations they have of their children. But God is not like that. He always leaves us free. But because he is perfect love, loving us more than we love ourselves, he, more than anyone, wants to see our full potential realised. And we have it in us to be like God himself. God has made us in his image, and we have the potential to become as loving as he is himself. This means that we cannot know God's love for us without at the same time knowing what he wants of us, which is to live a life of love. We can, if we like, call this a command, but, because that word now has such misleading overtones, it is perhaps better to see this aspect of God's love for us

82

as a pressing invitation. And on a number of occasions Jesus depicted the kingdom of God in terms of being invited to a Feast. The more we know how much God cares for us, the more pressing is his invitation that we begin to love others as he loves us.

HOW DO WE KNOW THE LORD'S WILL?

God has a purpose for us and he has revealed that purpose in Christ. This means that Christians have to take the idea of authority seriously. The Christian life is not something we have made up for ourselves. It is what God has shown us he wants.

The word 'authority' can be off-putting. It hints of repressive government or the establishment. But we might say of someone, 'He's the world's greatest authority on early maps', or, 'He has a natural authority'. The first judgement implies the possession of knowledge which we might wish to draw on. The second implies the possession of certain qualities. Both come together in spiritual matters, when we consider the kind of person that we might like to go to for spiritual guidance. We look for someone with a mind trained in a particular way and who has the qualities of integrity and holiness. We would go to them and be receptive of their wisdom and insight. God has this kind of authority. He has created a world and, through infinite wisdom and patience, is able to bring it to the consummation which perfect love has conceived for it. He thinks only of our good (and the good of all other persons) and is working night and day to bring it about. And all this is utterly natural to him. In thinking of us God is simply being himself, doing what we only experience in play. We recognise in God infinite wisdom, holiness and love. So his authority is intrinsic to his being. It is this authority that we recognise and to which we submit ourselves, that is, to which we seek to be as open, receptive and 'obedient' as possible.

Unfortunately Christians differ in their understanding of what God wants. All are agreed that it is in Christ himself that God shows us his heart and mind. The difficulty comes when we try to grasp, in human terms, just what this involves for us. Christians differ in what they regard as the ultimate authority for discerning the mind of Christ. But the following outline would command the support of many Christians today.

First, there is the authority of the Christian community led, as it believes, by the Holy Spirit. The first Christians had no Bible as we know it. They had the Jewish scriptures, which they interpreted as pointing to Christ. Then, as the original eyewitnesses of Jesus began to die, local churches put together sets of documents that they believed preserved the essentials of the faith. These writings would first have included letters written to the local church in question, and then any writings they had come across that had been intended for a wider Christian readership. These collections eventually came to be our New Testament. For some time there was doubt about exactly which writings should be included and which should be excluded. The Book of Revelation, for example, was not always included. But by the year 382 the New Testament as we know it had been given a seal of approval by the Church. Yet, in a way, it was not so much the Church conferring authority on these writings as recognising the authority that was inherent in them. A committee appointed to select pictures for an exhibition might say 'This one in', 'That one out'. But if they are presented with a masterpiece which they recognise, then that picture henceforth has an authoritative status that judges other lesser works. The Church existed before the Bible and we only have a

Bible because the Church under the Holy Spirit decreed that there should be one. But once the Bible had been formally recognised as authoritative it then existed as an authority over against the Christian community. The Church, being composed of fallible, sinful human beings, is always likely to go astray. The Bible remains as a touchstone and guide as to what is and what is not the mind of Christ.

The Bible has an intrinsic authority; but not apart from the Christian community out of whose life it arose. For the simple fact is, as Blake put it:

> Both read the Bible day and night,
> But thou read'st black where I read white.

This is why the tradition of the Church and in particular the great councils that were held in the early centuries are so important. In the first five hundred years of the Church there were many disputes, some of them crucial, such as whether Jesus was truly God, whether he had a human nature like ours, and so on. After a great deal of uncertainty the Church formulated its mind in seven ecumenical (universal) Councils. The decisions of these assemblies are not word for word true for all time. But the Holy Spirit is present in his Church and the conclusions can be taken as authoritative expressions of Christian truth.

At the time of these councils some Christians who could not agree with the decisions broke away and a number of the Churches they formed are still with us. Some of them, e.g. the large Coptic Church in Egypt, have in recent years been undergoing a powerful spiritual revival.

Since these first seven councils there have been two major cracks in the Church. The first was in 1054 when the Churches of the East, the Greek and Russian Orthodox Churches and others, split with the Church of the West, whose centre was at Rome. Then in the 16th century came the reformation, when many Churches in the West broke off from the Roman Catholic Church. Despite the movement for Christian unity, which has done much to draw Churches closer together, Christians today are often confused by this situation of competing authorities. It is not easy for someone to work out which is the true Church.

Throughout Christian history, but particularly since the Reformation, and particularly in America people have formed breakaway sects. To take just one example, the Irvingites in the nineteenth century decided to re-establish the primitive offices of the church, including having twelve apostles, in preparation for the near return of Christ. They had some success but have now almost died out. Because of this danger of groups setting up new self-styled churches the main body has always seen itself as 'catholic and apostolic', as the creed puts it. The word apostolic means that the Church must be the one descended from the apostles. One of the marks of this has been the presence of bishops who were consecrated by other bishops who themselves stood in the apostolic succession. The word catholic means universal and it indicates that the local church must be in communion with other churches in the world. A group of Christians who set themselves up as a new sect would not be at one with, or in communion with, Christians in other countries and in other ages. They are therefore outside the Catholic Church. The Roman Catholic Church, the Orthodox Churches and the Churches of the Anglican Communion all claim to be apostolic. This does not mean that the Churches of the Protestant Reformation are necessarily outside the Catholic Church. Obviously a Church in which the Bible is read, the sacraments are administered and the Gospel is preached is, in some important sense, a Church in the apostolic tradition. Yet until the reformation it was also considered essential for individual congregations to be in communion with a bishop who was himself in communion with other bishops.

Even Churches who claim to stand fully in the apostolic succession are not completely at one. This raises the question of a focus of unity for the Church as a whole, an ultimate source of authority. Certainly common sense, to put it no higher, demands such a focus. Historically the only contender for this role has been the Bishop of Rome. An important international commission composed of Roman Catholics and Anglicans dealing with this issue and referring to Rome, said, 'It seems appropriate that in any future union a universal primacy such as has been described should be held by that See.' This would probably be the position of the Orthodox Churches. Father Kallistos Ware, an Orthodox writer critical of claims of papal infallibility, has written, 'Orthodox in their turn need to take the idea of Primacy more seriously. Orthodox agree that the Pope is first among bishops: have they asked themselves carefully and searchingly what this really means?'

Many Roman Catholics now see the Papacy as a service of love offered for the unity of the church. Many other Christians are willing to accept the Pope in this sense for 'communion with him is intended as a safeguard of the catholicity of each local church and as a sign of the communion of all the churches'. But the question of primacy is at the moment inseparable from the question of infallibility. People, both within and outside the Roman Catholic Church, have debated what might be meant by this idea and in what sense if any it could be accepted. Hans Küng has written:

'The Church is distinguished from other human organisations — and this distinction is vital —

only by the promise given to it as the community of believers in Christ: the promise that it will survive all errors and sins, that its truth will remain imperishable and indestructible through all storms, that the message of Jesus Christ will endure in it, that Jesus Christ will remain with it in spirit and thus keep it in the truth through all errors and confusion . . . . The Church may forsake her God, he will not forsake her. On her path through time she may go astray, may stumble and often even fall, she may fall among thieves and be left lying for dead. Yet God will not abandon her . . . So the Church will continue on her way, living on the forgiveness, the healing and the strengthening of her Lord.'

At the moment this view is not accepted in the Roman Catholic Church as an adequate account of infallibility. If it ever were so accepted, Orthodox, Anglicans and even the most diehard Protestant should be able to rejoice. For what Küng is putting forward is nothing less, and nothing more, than wholehearted trust and confidence in Christ.

In so far as it is possible to sum up what is already a simplification of a complex and contentious area the following points might be made.

1   God has revealed himself and his purpose for us in Christ.

2   This revelation is authoritative. Christians try to discover what the will of the Lord is and do it.

3   The Bible has an intrinsic authority. It is a unique touchstone of what is and what is not of the mind of Christ.

4   The Bible cannot be separated from the Church out of whose life it arose and by whom it was accorded unique status. As the Holy Spirit guided

the Church in the formation of the canon, and in the seven ecumenical councils of the undivided Church, so he guides us today.

5   The Church of Christ is catholic and apostolic.
6   It may be that in the future the Bishop of Rome will be accepted by all parts of the Catholic Church as a focus of unity and an ultimate authority in cases of dispute.
7   The Church has erred in the past and will no doubt err in the future. But, despite the sins and failures of the Christian community, Christ remains with his people and the Church continues on her way 'living on the forgiveness, the healing and the strengthening of the Lord'.

INSTITUTION AND FELLOWSHIP

Either a person is brought up as a Christian and the truth of the faith takes hold of him from an early age, or he is converted later in life from indifference or unbelief. In either case he enters a community with a long tradition. Some people feel that the Church, considered as a traditional institution, is hostile to the Gospel. But there is nothing essentially unchristian about institutions. Institutions garner what is worthwhile from the past in order to conserve and hand it over to future generations. Any body which intends to expand through space or persist through time is bound to develop limbs. There must be ways of making decisions and conveying these decisions to the membership. There must be means of ensuring that the truth is taught to new generations. All this gives rise to buildings, decision-making bodies, facilities for training authorised teachers and so on. An institution can become an end in itself. It can become a hindrance to the Gospel and life in the Spirit. But were the

Church not an institution those who call themselves Christians would not have come to a saving faith. For it is the institutional aspect of the Church which enables the truth to be conveyed from generation to generation.

Because the Church exists to convey the truth of God's love to every creature under heaven it has inevitably developed as an organised body. But if it was only that, it would be dead. It needs above all to be a fellowship of the Spirit, a real community. There is a vivid description of the church in the Acts of the Apostles:

> 'They met constantly to hear the apostles teach, and to share the common life, to break bread, and to pray. A sense of awe was everywhere, and many marvels and signs were brought about through the apostles. All whose faith had drawn them together held everything in common: they would sell their property and possessions and make a general distribution as the need of each required. With one mind they kept up their daily attendance at the temple, and, breaking bread in private houses, shared their meals with unaffected joy, as they praised God and enjoyed the favour of the whole people. And day by day the Lord added to their number those whom he was saving.' (Acts 2. 42-47.)

This picture of the first Christians speaks for itself. Being a Christian is not something one does on one's own but in company with others in the fellowship of the Spirit. Where today can one discover a Christian community with a similar life about it? The best place to begin looking will be one of the small groups that now form part of the life of most congregations. For it is in a small group of about a dozen people who can meet on a regular basis for prayer, study and sharing of feelings, as well as thoughts, that a sense of the Church can develop. Such a group, perhaps a housegroup or study group or adult confirmation group that continues to meet, is small enough for its members to get to know one another and to develop a sense of trust. Such groups are not a substitute for the local congregation, but the congregation is usually too large for a sense of prayerful intimacy to develop. When, however, a congregation is composed of people who also belong to a small group, then it too begins to become a Christian community in the true sense.

The institutional and fellowship aspects of the Church are not essentially antagonistic to one another even though they often appear to be so in practice. When the life of the Church has been renewed small groups have usually had an important part to play, for example at the beginning of the Franciscan movement and in the early years of Methodism. Sometimes, as in the case of Methodism, the renewal has been so vigorous that the institution, in this case the Church of England, has not been able to contain it. But all charismatic renewal (renewal of God's gifts to us through his Spirit) runs into the sand unless the life it generates can be fed into the wider Church. On the other hand, one of the great strengths of the Roman Catholic Church, is that it can often allow renewal to take place without a great split. When a new religious movement like the Franciscans or the Jesuits gets officially recognised by the Pope, the renewal is contained within the Church as a whole and the Church as a whole is made fresh. This is an enormous advantage compared with Protestantism where renewal movements tend to start yet another denomination. There is a perfectly proper tension between the institution and the new life generated by the Holy Spirit. But the old bones and the new life need one another.

When faced with a decision even if it is comparatively small, for example whether to accept an invitation to go away for the weekend with a good friend when one has already accepted another invitation to do something at that time; but especially if it is momentous, for example whether or not to have an abortion, the believing Christian and the non-believer approach the matter from different points of view. The non-believer is concerned to do what is right. The Christian is also concerned to do what is right, but for him what is right is taken up into and defined by what the Lord wills for him. The Christian seeks the Lord's good pleasure. Day by day he prays, 'Thy will be done on earth as it is in heaven', and he has in mind the words of Jesus in the garden of Gethsemane, 'Thy will not mine be done'. This will of God is not something alien to us. It is not the wilful dictate of some stranger. God wills our good, he has our interests at heart even more than we have ourselves. So his will for us is identical with our own deepest desire for fulfilment and happiness. God's will and our striving for the complete realisation of our potential are coterminous. To embrace his will for us is to affirm our true being.

God's good purpose for us in the minutiae of everyday living has to be sought and struggled for in thought, prayer and love. But the heart of that purpose has been disclosed to us in Christ. The Christian life is based upon a recognition of that fact and a response to it. There are a number of claimants for the position of true interpreter of the mind of Christ, from 'The Bible and the Bible alone is the religion of protestants' on the one hand, to extreme ultramontanism (stress on the authority of the Pope) on the other. A possible view on this matter has been outlined. Through the Bible, and the tradition of the

Church as well as the common mind of the faithful in the contemporary world, we try to discover God's mind and will. This is not easy. Sometimes we are only aware of floundering around in the darkness. But we seek his will in order to respond to it. This response to what God has revealed of himself is not something we do on our own. We do it in company with other Christians, as a limb in Christ's body. Christians inevitably find, whether they like it or not, that they are part of the wider organised Church. So what becomes important in practice is to discover a local Christian congregation with an authentic spiritual life and a genuine sense of community.

Questions for discussion

1   Explore the idea that God's will for us and what we most deeply long for coincide.

2   Do you agree that Christians have to take the idea of authority seriously?

3   Take any decision with an ethical dimension, and explore the different ways in which a believer and a non-believer might try to work out what is the right thing to do.

4   How might a Christian group to which you belong become a greater source of support and strength to its members?

7

How to Pray

Prayer is crucial to the Christian life, indeed without it there is no Christian life. In chapter one it was suggested that God is not a piece of knowledge that we can stand over against and decide about in a detached way. We only know God by entering into relationship with him as our God.

In the last chapter it was said that at the heart of the Christian life is the attempt to discern God's will for us. This is impossible without prayer. This does not mean that prayer is easy. Most people who have tried to pray feel guilty and inadequate about their prayer life. Others have felt too shy or uninformed ever to begin praying seriously. But we have to start somewhere. Or if we have failed many times before, time and again we have to pick ourselves up and start again. For prayer and belief are most intimately linked. To believe is to pray and to cease to pray is to cease to have believed.

LISTENING

Sometimes we talk to our friends. At other times we listen to them. The same is true in our relationship with God. Most people tend to think of prayer as talking to God. But it is just as important to listen and because this is the aspect of prayer we most neglect it is here considered first.

When we are first introduced to someone we don't usually start chattering away to them about our own

1. I have written more fully on prayer in *Turning to Prayer* (Mowbrays).

concerns. We ask them about themselves and let them speak. So prayer should begin with a reverential pause, a realisation of who it is that one is in the presence of, God, the all-holy one. We kneel (or sit or stand), perhaps make the sign of the cross, and say, 'In the name of the Father and the Son and the Holy Spirit.' We remain silent for a few seconds before the awesome mystery of God. Then it is useful to read something, perhaps a passage from the Bible. The important point to remember is not to read too much. It may be necessary to read only a sentence, or a phrase or even a word. Read only until you discover a word or idea that you would like more time to think about or draw more deeply into yourself. Suppose for example you have started reading St Mark's Gospel, which begins, 'The beginning of the gospel of Jesus Christ, the Son of God'. The word gospel might arrest you. Knowing it means 'good news' this might start you wondering about the ways in which it comes to you as something good. Or it may be that the force of the words 'Son of God' strike you, but this time not so much as something to think about as words to pray. Having met a phrase or a word that interests you in some way, think about it, in particular its meaning for you. Then turn your thoughts, or the words, into a prayer. The simpler and shorter the prayer the better. For example the first verse of St Mark may lead you to pray 'Jesus, you are the Son of God' or 'Jesus, Son of God, help me to follow you today'. Then, having uttered this short prayer to God, be silent, with a wordless awareness that God is close to you. Be silent for about fifteen or thirty seconds and then when you find your mind wandering away, as most of us find happens, repeat the prayer again. The prayer brings your mind and heart back to God. Having said the prayer, remain in silence again. Repeat this pattern for a few minutes. Finally commend the day, or whatever it is that comes next, to

God and get on doing whatever has to be done.

When you come to God in this way bring a sense of expectation. God will share with you some insight into his mind and purpose. He will give you some grace or ask something of you. Perhaps all three, for they are intertwined. You have made yourself available to God and he will assuredly bless you. Do not try to make yourself feel religious feelings. What you feel does not matter. The important thing is to try to wait with quiet attentiveness on God, simply being aware of his presence in and through all things. He is close to us all the time, whether we are aware of it or not.

Many people, perhaps most of us, find that trying to be aware of the presence of God is difficult or unreal. We are aware of our surroundings and of ourselves, but of nothing else. Any attempt to make oneself feel aware of something else seems artificial. We are conscious not of a divine presence but of an absence. But perhaps this is as it should be. For if God is not a thing amongst other things, whether in the world of stones or ghosts, then to be aware of this is to begin to know him as he really is. There is an important sense in which God can only be present in his world under the form of absence; and this means that an awareness of his absence is also a dawning awareness of his presence. But there are other senses in which God is present in his world. After all he is its creative ground. He is the fount from whom every electron, every molecule, every self flows. When we come to pray and become aware of what is before our eyes, we can remind ourselves of this and simply wait in stillness.

Some people would like to use the Bible for this simple form of meditation and contemplation but do not know where to begin. Several organizations and publishers provide notes to aid people with reading the Bible. You may browse in a religious bookstore to see what is available. A Christian friend may have a suggestion from his or her own experience. A priest or pastor may provide helpful resources. You may prefer an aid in which the text of the Bible to be meditated on is printed in full. This is handy because you do not have to have a Bible with you. Such an aid can be slipped into a briefcase or hand-bag and read on a bus or during lunchtime.

Reading the Bible for meditation and contemplation should be distinguished from two other uses of the Bible. Sometimes people like to read a great chunk at a time, for example a letter of St Paul, in order to take in the whole sweep of his argument. With meditation the point is to pray rather than to read. The less one reads and the more one prays the better. At other times a person who is interested in the Bible can read it with the aid of a commentary. This can be very useful. A critical, scholarly approach to the Bible, though in one way it makes the Bible more difficult for people, can also bring all kinds of illumination. For although a critical study of the Bible can, in the early stages, undermine a simple faith it can also bring deeper conviction and a larger understanding of God. But again, this activity should be distinguished from what has been described. Reading a commentary is a useful optional extra for those with the time and the inclination. Meditation is essential to the Christian life. It forms part of the bare minimum of a Christian life style.

What has been said applies to people who genuinely want to use the Bible for meditation and contemplation. Others, perhaps because they had the Bible taught to them at school before they had any inward conviction or feel for its beliefs, find the Bible difficult or boring or both. If you feel like this it is much better to use some other book as a basis for your meditation, for example one of the great spiritual classics, such as *The Cloud of Unknowing* or Julian of

Norwich's *Revelations of Divine Love*. Many of these classics are available in cheap paperback. The principles already outlined apply if one of these books is used. Read only until some truth begins to take hold of the mind. Focus on some word or idea that you would like to think about more deeply and then draw into yourself. Some modern books of prayers or meditations can equally well be used.

If the thought of reading the Bible fills you with a heavy feeling, there is no point in forcing yourself to read it. The Bible is absorbing and thrilling. But we need to discover this for ourselves and will do so when the time is right. You will find that as your Christian life develops under the Holy Spirit you will discover a 'right' book to be reading at each particular time. Our being is ready to receive a particular truth, and only that truth, and the right book or talk or sermon will appear at the right moment to enable it to do so. Each one of us is different and at a different stage of our Christian life. This raises the question of spiritual guidance. In the well known story of Samuel as a boy in the Temple (I Samuel 3. 1-10) the Lord calls Samuel three times, 'Samuel, Samuel.' But it was only through the ministry of Eli who interpreted this call as the call of God, that Samuel came to say, 'Speak, for thy servant hears'. It is desirable to have someone to whom we can turn for spiritual direction and help. In the first Christian centuries this person was sometimes called a 'soul-friend'. This spiritual guide can be a local priest or minister, or a monk, or he (or she) might be a Christian friend of spiritual discernment and wisdom. For some people the idea of having an official spiritual guide sounds much too formal and formidable. Instead of going as a pupil to some expert whom they do not know well, they prefer to both give to and receive from a close friend with similar beliefs. For them spiritual insight and growth come above all in the context of friendship and mutual sharing. This person is able to help us draw closer to God. The Christian life is not a static life. The Holy Spirit is always leading us into new insights and a more committed discipleship. A 'soul-friend' can help us understand these promptings and leadings of the Spirit, as they are mediated to us through the ups and downs, the crises and changes of our lives.

THE ELEMENTS OF PRAYER

Waiting upon God, just being with him and trying to be sensitive to the leading of his Spirit is an essential part of prayer. So too is speaking to God. It is said that Moses spoke to God face to face as a man speaks with his friend. This is how Christians relate to God − as a friend. But if we spent the whole time asking one of our human friends for things it would be an odd relationship. Yet for some people prayer to God seems mostly to consist of just this. So it is good to check that the following elements all have a place in our friendship with God.

THANKSGIVING

It was suggested in the last chapter that the Christian life is one of recognition and response. We have some insight, however small, into God's great love for us and we desire to respond to this. This response is one of gratitude and will naturally express itself in prayers of thanks. It is good to end the day by reflecting on its experiences and saying thank you to God for what one has appreciated. It is easy to thank God for flowers or a nice day or a special treat. We need to learn to give thanks for so many things that we usually take for granted, for the qualities in people around us and for the special and distinctive blessings that come to us through our life as a Christian. When, for example, did one last thank God for particular qualities in a colleague at work? If we pray for the conversion of our unbelieving friends it might be better to thank God for that of God which, unknown to them, is already reflected in their lives. Too often we pray for someone who is sick, without, if they get well, thanking God afterwards. How infrequently do we thank God for the opportunity to pray to him or worship him? Paul begins nearly all his letters with an expression of thanks to God. Even to the church at Corinth, beset as it was with troubles, he begins, 'I give thanks to God always for you because of the grace of God which was given you in Christ Jesus.'

PRAISE

Praise is simply telling someone the good things you have noticed about them. 'That's a lovely dress,' 'What a marvellous meal — you are a good cook.' It arises naturally out of thanksgiving. When we thank God, it is for something he has given. When we praise him we focus on him in himself. 'O God you are good, all good, supreme good.' Praise to God can arise spontaneously in one's own words. It is also useful to know by heart phrases from the psalms or the liturgy, so that when our own emotions are damped down the words of others can lift us beyond ourselves and so that when our emotions are high they find an easy and natural expression in praise. For example, on seeing a tree in blossom our natural reaction is to say, 'How lovely'. The person steeped in God might say, just as naturally, 'Praise the Lord, O my soul, all that is within me praise his holy name'.

Because we are made in God's image we are capable of recognising good and evil and of choosing between them. During the last century we have become aware of just how limited our freedom is. Nevertheless, within limits, we are free. This means we can assume responsibility for our behaviour and, if we come to think something we have done is wrong, say sorry. Most of us find it difficult to say sorry either to another person or to God. Or we always say, 'I'm sorry *but . . .*' Our pride and natural defensiveness resist making ourselves so vulnerable. Nevertheless, self-examination should play a part in our relationship with God. This should go deeper than simply asking what we have done wrong. We need to become aware of the unconscious feelings which lead us to act in particular ways. We can do this by being 'mindful' as the Buddhists say, being aware of how we react in particular situations. How do we react to authority figures, for example? If we find within ourselves an expressive desire to gain approval, what is there within us which needs recognising and affirming? How do we react to our peers? If it is with excessive competitiveness, jealousy or criticism, what is there within us that needs taking into the open and looking at? Our daydreams are a good guide to some aspect of ourselves that we have not yet fully become conscious of. We have daydreams of escape, fantasies of revenge, mental scenarios in which we imagine ourselves in an important position, others in which we are full of self-pity or resentment. These all tell us something about ourselves — not something which needs blaming, but something which needs making friends with. It has been said that each one of us needs to act as an adult to the child within us. A great deal of the behaviour that we dislike in ourselves comes from the child within wanting to be taken notice of. We need to make friends with that inner child, hold him or her by the hand, and lead him into the friendly, accepting light of day. Even when the child within us wants to say or do something totally unacceptable from a rational and moral point of view, there is usually something within us which, before anything else, needs understanding and accepting.

Self-examination has two parts. We attempt to discover actions or deliberate nursing of feelings for which we feel sorry and for which we can be held responsible. Our contrition can be expressed in private prayer to God, in the general confession in worship, or in confession before a priest. The Church of England's attitude to private confession is that 'All may, none must, some should'. It is available for people whose sins are lying heavy on the conscience and, just as important, as a regular spiritual discipline for anyone taking the life of discipleship seriously. For some people the person to whom they go for spiritual direction is also the person to whom they go to make their confession. It is much easier to mumble one's sins into the eiderdown than it is to write them down and read them out before a priest acting as a representative of God and the Christian community, but to do the latter is a mark of seriousness in the attempt to follow Christ. In his journals Kierkegaard said that at the Reformation the abolition of confession by Protestant churches was the joint work of priest and people . . . 'it made religion all too real'. A wise 'soul-friend' or confessor will help a person recognise and accept the rejected bits of himself or herself that come out in feelings of vanity, resentment, self-pity and so on. Through talking to such a person the forgiveness of God is mediated to us in two ways; through the formal act of absolution or forgiveness uttered by the priest; and through his acceptance of the whole of us, warts and all, shaming feelings as well as what we think of as pious ones, as we talk to him honestly about ourselves and our struggles as a Christian.

PRAYING FOR OTHERS

Praying for other people is utterly natural. Intercession, as praying for others is sometimes called, often gives rise to difficulties. If God knows what we want, why bother to tell him? Surely he is doing all he can to help anyway, so what difference does prayer make? But despite all these questions we persist, rightly, in praying for others because we care for them. We bring to God what is in our heart and so we bring to him those we love and their particular needs.

It is true that before we pray for someone God is doing all he can for them. But it is God's chosen way to achieve his purpose only with our co-operation. He does not bulldoze his way through us. He works always in and through the wills of those who make themselves available for his work. And he works not only through what we do but through our prayers. When we pray for others we simply lift them into the presence of God. We hold up their needs before him. God works through our prayers, as he works through the prayers of the saints, to meet the needs of those for whom we pray. From the practical point of view we need, as Christians, to widen the circle of those for whom we pray. It is easy to pray for our family. But we need to lift into his presence as wide a range of human needs and people as we can manage.

Real prayer should not just consist in the repetition of a name. Sometimes it requires hard thought to discover just what it is that we should be praying for in relation to a particular person. We need to think about the person and ask ourselves before God, as honestly as possible, what we should pray for. This applies to all prayer. Before we pray, we need to pray that we may pray according to the mind of Christ. For true prayer is the prayer of Christ in and through us. This is present when our little prayer and Christ's prayer are at one.

GOD AND ME

The fifth element in prayer is ones own relationship to God, including one's own needs. The golden rule here is to be as honest as possible. The person God wants is the real me. Even though I may feel angry or resentful or sorry for myself, he would rather have that me than a pious fraud. So we can tell God just what we are feeling. Nor should we be ashamed to bring our wants before God, however trivial they might seem. Everyone is a bundle of wants and if we are bringing the whole person before God, which is what he wants, then those needs and desires must be included. The prayer of Jesus in the Garden of Gethsemane is a model. He brought his real feelings, 'Father, take this cup from me'. But he moved beyond this to surrender himself to the Father's will, whatever it might turn out to be: 'Nevertheless not my will but thine be done.'

For some people prayer is not so much a colloquy with God as a matter of 'centring down.' God is immanent, within us at the depth of our being, and prayer can be understood as an attempt to be more aware of this. One simple way of beginning to do this is to say slowly, several times, with ample use of silence, the famous prayer:

> God be in my head, and in my understanding;
> God be in my eyes, and in my looking;
> God be in my mouth, and in my speaking;
> God be in my heart, and in my thinking;
> God be at mine end, and at my departing.

These five elements of prayer can be included in any set time of prayer that we may have. They can also arise naturally out of the experiences of the day. There are many good experiences during each day for which we can give thanks. Sadly, for many people, there is little or no connection between their religion and the experiences in life which they most enjoy. All that interests, excites and makes us feel good to be alive should be integrated into our religion. If we enjoy sport, we can give thanks for the fitness of our bodies and the sense of well being after exercise. If we enjoy watching a TV programme we can give thanks for the illumination or pleasure it brings. If we enjoy a glass of beer in a pub this, just as much as the sight of a daffodil in spring, is something for which we give thanks. There is no pleasure in life too ordinary or secular for thanks to be said to God.

The day contains not only good experiences but also moments of need or exhaustion. These too can be turned into prayers. For example, the physical act of sitting in a chair or relaxing in one's bath at the end of the day, can be turned into a prayer of letting go into God. The sight of other people in the tube train or on a bus can give rise to prayers of thanks and intercession for them.

The prayer of a Christian is meant to be unceasing. This does not mean that we have to think about God all the time. For most of the time we are meant to concentrate on the job in hand. It does mean trying to be aware of God's presence in those odd moments which would otherwise be wasted. This can be achieved in two overlapping and mutually reinforcing ways. From out of one's period of silence and listening to God we can take a particular word or prayer. This is carried into the day and from time to time we become aware of it. The word or prayer can, if necessary, be written down, either in a special notebook we keep for the purpose or in the pages of our ordinary diary. For example, suppose that in our period of meditation we have used the phrase, 'Truly my soul waiteth still upon thee, O Lord' (based on a phrase in Psalm 62) then in the odd moments of waiting during the day — waiting for a train to come, waiting in a queue, waiting for someone to come through the door, waiting for the person to answer at the other end of the telephone — this phrase can be used. Periods of waiting, of which the day is full, can be turned into moments of waiting upon God. We can take something from our period of meditation to carry with us through the day. On the other hand, the day itself gives rise to a variety of experiences, gratitude, need, frustration, exhaustion, bitterness, love and hate, all of which can be turned into prayer. The Christian ideal is to pray without ceasing. A silent waiting upon God in a set time of prayer permeates the day from one end. The multiplicity of experiences which the day brings forth are lifted into prayer from the other. The result is that prayer and life are integrated and we stand as a whole person before God.

OUR OWN WORDS AND THOSE OF OTHER PEOPLE

It is important to use our own words in prayer. God wants us to come before him as the person we really are, and that means with the words which arise in our heart. But it is good also to use other people's words. There are three reasons for this. First, whenever we pray we do not pray alone. We pray as part of the Church. Whenever or wherever we pray we are one with the fellowship of Christians stretching back through time and extending outwards into the world. To use one of the prayers from the liturgy of the

Church or one of the great prayers of past Christians is a sign of union with other Christians. This is particularly so of course of the Lord's Prayer. Second, our own prayers often become thin and dry. Often, particularly in the mornings, it is difficult to get anything out of ourselves except a confused sleepiness. If we use a set form of prayer then we get straight into the business of praying without being dragged back by our own inertia. This point applies particularly to acts of praise, which do not usually come naturally. It can help to use part of the Te Deum, 'We praise Thee O God, we acknowledge Thee to be the Lord, all the earth doth worship Thee', or part of the Gloria from the Eucharist. The third reason is that the tried prayers of other Christians have an educative effect upon us. They not only take us beyond ourselves when we are not particularly in the mood for prayer, they can also become material for meditation. Instead of reading a bit of the Bible or another book, we can take someone else's prayer to think about and pray slowly. Even if we are not using the prayer in this way, as a basis for meditation, the sheer act of using it educates the soul.

TIMES AND PLACES

Keeping friendships in repair, whether with our fellow human beings or with God, means giving time to it. This means taking a close and realistic look at one's pattern of life and seeing when this might be. Millions of Christians set aside time each day before they start work. Others, because of family commitments then or because they are too sleepy, find this a bad time. Two dangers need to be avoided. First, leaving it until one feels like it. Although spontaneous prayer, arising out of the experiences of the day is important, something more regular than this is also needed. Most people seem to be so busy that, unless a period of prayer is built into the rhythm of the day or week as a matter of course, it gets pushed out. The other danger is to be too ambitious. If a person just embarking on the life of the spirit for the first time says, 'I am going to spend two hours a day in meditation and prayer', they are likely to find it beyond them. Be realistic. Decide what you honestly want to do and what you can, without too much strain on the other members of the household, fit into your life. Then offer this to God. 'God, I want to spend time each day with you. Help me to find ten minutes.' If it is possible to put aside time for prayer in the early part of the day this is, in one way, better than the end, for it sets the whole day going in the right spirit.

Sadly few churches are kept open for prayer, for a church is the obvious place to pray in. But there may be one near home or it may be possible to pop into one during a lunch hour. If a person prays at home, as most people do, it can be helpful to have a special spot in the room or house, perhaps with a picture or a crucifix, as an aid to recollection. If we have a special bit of space in our lives it can help us keep a special time. If we have a special time, then all time will become special.

Everyone who prays is conscious of failure. Often we do not carry out the bare minimum that we set ourselves. This is one of the reasons why the Church's year is helpful. It provides seasons such as Advent and Lent where we can take a look at ourselves and start again. A monk was once asked what he did in his monastery all day and he replied, 'We fall and get up again, fall and get up again, fall and get up again.' So it is with all of us. Prayer is often the first thing to be edged out of our life. Instead of being top priority it often comes last. That is why we need a realistic self-discipline. This discipline is not something imposed on us from outside. Rather, in our deepest moments, we ask ourselves what we really want. We then allow what we have decided in those moments to shape the pattern of the rest of our life. In our deepest moments we know that prayer, being close to God, is the most important thing in life, so we decide to set aside a particular period each day, or a certain number of periods each week. This is what we *really* want, and we allow what we really want to support our fluctuating feelings at other times. But we still fail and need, many times, to pick ourselves up and start again. This is why it is an advantage to have someone to talk to about spiritual matters. It is an added incentive to take stock and start anew.

However much of a failure we feel ourselves to be, God is present with us; and at any moment we can turn away from ourselves and our sense of failure to rejoice in him. This is of crucial importance. Some people feel such a failure they push God even further away. But at any moment of any day we can lift our eyes to him and he is there ready waiting to embrace us. Indeed, paradoxically, when we turn to God out of the mess of our life we seem to be closer to him than when things are going smoothly. At any time we can simply turn to God and say, 'Lord, I've hardly thought of you all week, hardly said a prayer. Yet I know you have been with me and are with me now . . .'

Questions for discussion

1   What experiences in life do you really enjoy but don't give thanks for — perhaps because of a too narrow view of religion?

2   This chapter has mainly discussed prayer in terms of a relationship with God. What ways of prayer are

there which help us to discover and live from God within us?

3 What parts of yourself do you find most unacceptable? How far are you able to accept and give thanks for the fact that this is all part of the God-given you?

4 What words from other people's prayers do you find most helpful for your own?

8

The Meaning of the Eucharist

WHY SACRAMENTS?

The 1662 Prayer Book defined a sacrament as 'an outward and visible sign of an inward and spiritual grace'. In trying to understand the place of sacraments within the purpose of God it helps to bear in mind three points. First, we live in a sacramental universe. Everything that exists, all material things, reveal and body forth some aspect of the divine glory.

> The world is charged with the grandeur of God.
> It will flame out, like shining from shook foil.

Nearly all human beings receive refreshment from nature. Some people cannot survive unless they get out into the country from time to time for a walk. Others feel emotionally and spiritually deprived if they are not in contact with trees or flowers. Nature is God's nature. It only exists because he holds it in being. Through this nature the renewing and quickening life of God himself is imparted to us. This is true even though 'all is seared with trade; bleared, smeared with toil', because, as Hopkins continues, 'There lives the dearest freshness deep down things'. The Holy Spirit is present vivifying nature, and, through nature, us.

Second, we are not disembodied spirits. We are a unity of body, mind and spirit. We do not for the most part communicate with one another telepathically, directly from mind to mind. We use certain outward gestures of face and hands, sound waves set up in the air which beat upon our ear. This view of man as a

111

psychosomatic unity, as well as being natural to modern man, is very much a Hebrew view. For the People of the Old Testament man was not a soul imprisoned in a fleshly body. He was flesh that had been breathed into, brought to conscious spiritual life, by the Spirit of God.

Third, a distinction can be drawn between artificial signs and natural signs. With an artificial sign there is no necessary connection between the sign and what it signifies. For example the letter X means one thing if it appears on a road sign, another if it comes at the bottom of a letter, yet something else if it appears in a mathematics book. The meaning is what human beings choose to make it mean in a given context. With natural signs, however, there is a close, even integral, connection between the sign and the thing signified. The sign or symbol is itself an instance of the thing signified. The meaning of a kiss for example does not depend on what different cultures choose to make it mean, as though in one place it could express hate and in another indifference. It is in all cultures a natural expression of friendship. It is both a sign of love and an expression of that love.

Against the background of these three points — that matter is fundamentally good and can be used by God for his purposes, that man is a psychosomatic unity and we communicate with one another through outward visible things, and that natural signs are themselves an instance of what they signify — sacraments are entirely natural. God takes certain material things, the water of Baptism, the bread and wine of the Holy Communion, first to cleanse us and join us to himself and then to feed us with his new life and love in Christ. Baptism and Holy Communion are the two main sacraments. In traditional catholic theology there are another five, lesser sacraments: confirmation, matrimony, penance, ordination and unction (annointing a person with oil when they are sick or close to death). Quakers, like the Salvation Army, do not have sacraments in a special sense but they try to see everything, particularly all meals, as sacramental.

THE DIVINE BANQUET

Meals are not just a means of obtaining enough calories and proteins to live on. Sitting round a table together focuses and kindles life as it is meant to be. However difficult it may be in the modern world with so much rush, television and the disintegration of family life, most families still try to sit down together as a family from time to time. On those occasions the atmosphere is important and can be very special, for we imbibe not just the food but the whole atmosphere of the meal. The meal can be a focus of all that we most love about life — a group of people, the family, a friend or two, one of whom perhaps is having a hard time, sitting round a table, relaxed, laughing, talking, enjoying one another's company.

Meals together, table fellowship, were even more important to the Jews of old than they are to us. The intimate meals that Jesus shared with his disciples would have been an important part of their life together. Because of this importance of fellowship with one another at table it was natural to think of the coming kingdom of God as a great banquet. This image played an important part in the thinking of Jesus. As he went about asking people to change their whole outlook and enter his father's kingdom he said it was like inviting people to a party.

> 'A man once gave a great banquet, and invited many; and at the time for the banquet he sent his servant to say to those who had been invited, "Come; for all is now ready." ' (Luke 14.16.)

Jesus never ceased to be amazed that the so called religious refused the invitation he gave them. On the other hand those whose experience had forced them to shed all illusions about themselves accepted the invitation with alacrity. It would still be a marvellous, joyous occasion.

> 'Many will come from east and west and sit at table with Abraham, Isaac, and Jacob in the kingdom of heaven.' (Matt. 8.11.)

So it was that on the last occasion that Jesus sat down to a meal with his friends he looked back not only to the meals they had shared together on the way, not only to the great passover meals when they remembered and celebrated God's deliverance of his people from Egypt, but he looked forward also to the time when mankind would be freed from sin and death and would sit down at the divine banquet of the new age.

> 'I tell you that I shall not drink again of this fruit of the vine until that day when I drink it new with you in my Father's kingdom.' (Matthew 26.29.)

The Eucharist is first of all a meal. It is not an ordinary meal but a symbolic meal, a sign of what will ultimately be. It looks back to the Last Supper, the meals Jesus shared with his friends and the Passover celebrations. But even more it looks forward to that time when all things will be made new in the kingdom. It is an anticipation of that final state of affairs when mankind will be so united in love with one another and with God that they will sit at the heavenly banquet together. Christian people breaking bread together, whether it is at a house Mass or in a cathedral, are a sign of what God has in mind for the whole of humanity. Theirs is a foretaste of the unity of all God's creation bound together in love and joy and peace.

All Christians believe that Christ is present at the Eucharist. No Christian believes in his 'real absence'. We do not just sit down at table with one another with the host absent. The host is present making the occasion all that it is. But the presence of Christ is not a localised presence like sticks and stones with their clear outlines or boundaries, indicating where one thing ends and another thing begins. Christ is present as God is present; in all things, but in all things in various ways and under different forms. Christ is present in all things as the power which holds them in being. Without his creating, sustaining presence everything would collapse into nothingness. Then Christ is also present in everything through his boundless capacity to enter sympathetically into every situation by the power of imaginative love. If our tiny, limited and flawed love can do this how much more can divine love, unlimited by time or space, unmarred by the slightest trace of self-absorption, enter into the being of every particle of creation. Christ is not identical with the creation. He is utterly other than the created world; he transcends it, to use the technical word; but just because of this he is able to enter into it at every point by the power of divine love taken to the uttermost. There are other ways too in which Christ is 'in' his creation. He is, as it were, formed within it, in the lives of those individuals and groups which consciously seek to be of one mind with his Father. Christ is in the hearts of all people, but obviously the life of a good person reveals God more than that of an evil person, and a saint, whose life is transparent to God in a way that others are not yet, gives a still clearer manifestation of the divine presence.

For Christ plays in ten thousand places,
Lovely in limbs, and lovely in eyes not his
To the Father through the features of men's faces.

According to the Gospels Christ is present in an
especially intense way when Christian people meet
together in faith. 'Where two or three are gathered in
my name, there am I in the midst of them.' Therefore
when it is asserted that Christ is present in the
Eucharist, or that he is sacramentally present in the
bread and wine, this is not a question of an absent
Christ suddenly being present. Christ is always present
with his people, 'Lo, I am with you always, to the end
of time,' but he is present in different ways under
different forms. Through his Spirit he is present
speaking to his people when the Bible is read and the
Gospel proclaimed. He is present in those in need,
whether those needs are being met or ignored.
(Matthew 25.31 to end.) He is also present in the bread
and wine of the Eucharist. The bread and wine
become the life of Christ, the food of angels, with
which Christ feeds our soul. They become, in a
spiritual way, his 'Body and Blood.'

For people who have not been brought up within the
Christian Church and for all of us when we stop and
think about it, the idea of partaking of the body and
blood of Christ is startling and perhaps horrifying.
These words refer of course to something spiritual,
Christ himself, his divine life, love and peace. But the
phrases 'the body of Christ' and 'the blood of Christ'
cannot be ignored. First, they are the words which
appear in the Gospels. 'Take, eat; this is my body',
and, 'This is my blood of the covenant', are the words
which appear in St Matthew's Gospel for example:
Second, these words, so beautiful yet so brutal, remind
us that the one who gives himself to us lived out his life
in human conditions like ours. His body was broken

116

and his blood shed, in order to bring us into a true relationship with his Father.

The word transubstantiation has usually been used in the Roman Catholic Church to indicate that the inner reality of the bread and wine in the Eucharist are really changed. This word derives from a philosophy which distinguished between accidents i.e. the taste, texture and smell of bread, and its substance i.e. the 'breadiness' of bread. According to the doctrine of transubstantiation the accidents of the bread remained the same whilst its inner substance or essence was changed into the body and blood of Christ. Modern philosophers do not find it easy to make sense of the distinction between the accidents and the substance of an object, or at least they do not work naturally with such a distinction. So an important footnote to the joint statement on the Eucharist drawn up by an international commission of Anglican and Roman Catholic scholars says, 'the term should be seen as affirming the fact of Christ's presence and of the mysterious and radical change which takes place. In contemporary Roman Catholic theology it is not understood as explaining *how* the change takes place.'

In the Eucharist, as the joint statement puts it, 'Christ's body and blood become really present and are really given.' How can this be so? Three points need to be borne in mind. First, any object can, quite rightly, be described from a number of different points of view. Put a child in a circle consisting of an atomic physicist, a biochemist, a geneticist, a psychologist, an historian, a sociologist, a poet and a theologian, and the child will be described from the point of view of his biochemistry, his genetic make-up, his place in the family and so on. These descriptions will be complementary rather than mutually exclusive. Nor can it be held that one description is more important or all embracing than others. Some people have a

117

tendency to describe scenes in the most basic terms. But if, for example, Dennis Brain's horn playing is described in terms of air being pushed through metal or Solzhenitsyn's speeches are described in terms of his personal psychology, the deeper significance and meaning of the playing and the speeches will be missed.

Second, the significance and meaning of any event can only rightly be judged in its context. What Solzhenitsyn says can only be understood against the background of the history of Russia, the rise of Communism, the changes happening in the western world and so on. It is within this wide context that we have to try to assess the meaning and importance of what he is saying. Or, to take another example, if a person described a sharp length of metal coming down to rest on the shoulder of a kneeling man it could mean many things. But if we then saw the context in which this took place, a state room with a crowned figure in it, and heard the words 'I dub thee Sir . . .', we would immediately know the meaning and importance of what was happening.

Third, the true significance of any event can only be known at the end of time, when the whole infinitely complex and detailed pattern of history can be seen as a piece. Historians in each age continually reassess the past and reinterpret what has happened in the light of new facts, subsequent events and a wider perspective. Only at the end of history, when it is seen from the vantage point of its purpose and goal in the eyes of God, will the true significance of any event be known. Christians believe that the end of history, its meaning and purpose, have been made present in Christ. At the Last Supper, thinking of his inevitable death the next day, and knowing it would be the last time he would break bread with them, Jesus said those mysterious words over the bread and wine. There is a rhyme, attributed to Queen Elizabeth I, which goes:

Twas God the Word that spake it,
He took the bread and brake it;
And what the Word did make it
That I believe and take it

At first glance this verse appears to express an evasive agnosticism about what actually happens in the Eucharist. At another level it reveals an understanding both simple and profound. The ultimate meaning of things is known to God alone. But his eternal Word has become incarnate in Christ and the human words of that Word disclose to us the heart and mind of God. Anything which has God in it has an abyss of mystery in it. We can never have the meaning of the Eucharist 'buttoned-up'. But because 'Twas God the Word that spake it', we can trust him and trust that through the bread and wine he gives us himself.

THE EUCHARIST AS AN OFFERING

The Eucharist is a symbolic meal, a foretaste of the divine banquet in which all the faithful will share. But it is not only with one another that we sit down (or kneel, or stand). Christ himself is present feeding us heavenly food, his own God-life, his body broken and his blood shed for us. The Eucharist is also an offering and people sometimes talk of 'the sacrifice of the Mass'. Protestants do not like this phrase because it seems to imply a repetition of the unique sacrifice of Christ on the cross. The appropriate sentences in the joint statement need therefore to be heeded by all who have either attacked or defended the phrase 'the sacrifice of the Mass'.

'Christ's redeeming death and resurrection took place once and for all in history. Christ's death on the cross, the culmination of his whole life of obedience, was the one, perfect and sufficient sacrifice for the sins of the world. There can be no repetition of or addition to what was then accomplished once for all by Christ. Any attempt to express a nexus between the sacrifice of Christ and the Eucharist must not obscure this fundamental fact of the Christian faith.'

The Christ who is present at the Eucharist is the second person of the Holy Trinity. Within the Godhead the Father eternally pours himself out to the Son and the Son eternally responds with an act of perfect trust and love. What happened during the incarnation was that this response of the Son to the Father within the life of the Godhead was worked out in human terms. It is true that we only know that the life of the Trinity is one of mutual giving and receiving because of what Jesus revealed. But what he revealed, the life of one who prayed to and received from, the one he called Abba, is a segment in time and space of what continues eternally. Therefore the Christ who is present at the Eucharist is the Christ who eternally receives from and offers himself back to the Father. His presence is not static, but living and dynamic, a never ending movement lifting the things of earth to heaven.

It is often pointed out that when the Jews of old remembered the great events of their history and the Passover they did not think of this solely in terms of a mental happening. The deliverance of Egypt was somehow made present again; the experience was relived. The 'remembering' of Christ's death and resurrection at the Eucharist is of the same kind. It is not a bare mental event. Rather, what happened in the past is vividly present. This happens because all history is contained within God, and Christ's sacrificial life and death were a working out in human terms of the eternal offering of the Son to the Father. God is present at the Eucharist, the God whose son was incarnate in Jesus. Both the eternal dimension and the historical dimension are important. Without God's eternity what happens in history would disappear for ever without recall. But we only know what happens in God's eternity because of what actually took place in the life, death and resurrection of Christ, and through these events the human and historical are taken up into the life of God himself. At the Eucharist we remember something very specific and historical, Christ who died and rose again. But we 'remember' the cross and resurrection within the God whose life those events reveal and through whom they are present again.

The whole Eucharist is an offering, but this has three aspects which are focused at different points.

First, at the offertory when the bread and wine are taken, often from the back of the church by lay people, and laid on the table. In this action the Christian makes himself and all that he is, available for God, flawed and imperfect though he knows himself to be. 'There are you on the altar, there are you in the chalice', as St. Augustine used to tell the Christians that he was instructing. Strictly, of course, we have nothing to offer, or, as one prayer puts it, 'I offer Thee the one thing I really possess, my capacity for being filled by Thee'.

Second, shortly after the words of consecration when we celebrate and proclaim the death and resurrection of Christ, we reflect on Christ's offering of himself to the Father. As the third of the Eucharistic prayers in the Roman Catholic missal puts it, 'we offer you in thanksgiving this holy and living sacrifice'. Towards the end of the main thanksgiving prayer the priest will often raise the host (a piece of the consecrated bread) and the chalice. This provides a visible focus for the eternal offering of the Son to the Father, worked out in the life and death of Christ and now made present in the Eucharist, raising our feeble self-offering heavenwards.

Third, after receiving Holy Communion, Christians will once more make themselves available for Christ's work. United with Christ through the Holy Communion, taken up into his eternal self-offering, we offer ourselves once again. We open ourselves to God that his purpose may be accomplished in and through us.

HOW OFTEN AND HOW?

There are a number of different names for the same service, Mass, Holy Communion, the Lord's Supper, the Breaking of Bread, the Eucharist. The name is not important. What matters is that from the first days of the Christian Church this service has been at the centre of the Christian life. As Acts 2.42 puts it, 'They devoted themselves to the apostles' teaching and fellowship, to the breaking of bread and the prayers'. In recent years the word Eucharist (from a Greek word meaning thanksgiving) has become a popular name for the service, for it does not arouse the prejudices of words like Mass or Holy Communion. The use of this word reflects the fact that there is now a wide measure of agreement on this service and that the controversies of the Reformation period are being put behind. This chapter has quoted from the Agreed Statement on the Eucharist. This was signed not only by leading Roman Catholics and catholic minded Anglicans but by people in the evangelical tradition as well.

It is now widely agreed that the natural and proper thing for Christians to do is to join with other believers in doing what the Lord said ('Do this in remembrance of me') on the day of the resurrection (Sunday). Indeed a period of daily private prayer and a weekly attendance at the Eucharist would seem to constitute the basic minimum of a Christian life-style. These are the essential signs of our desire to love God and our neighbour and the means by which we receive the grace to do so. In addition to joining with other believers at the Eucharist on Sundays and days such as Christmas Day, Maundy Thursday, Good Friday and Ascension Day are normally regarded as days when a Christian should join in the worship of God with other Christians. These are sometimes called solemnities or principal holy days. Next in order of importance are festivals or greater holy days, such as Epiphany, and the feasts of the Apostles, when it is good to be present at the Eucharist if one can. In addition to this there may be a service of Holy Communion or Mass on every day of the week. In a country like Poland the churches overflow with people on ordinary weekdays. In South Africa priests have noted that there will sometimes be a hundred or so people at the 5.30 a.m. Mass on weekdays, black people who would then have to walk miles to work. Sadly, since the seventeenth century, (with the partial exception of the last quarter of Queen Victoria's reign) English people have accepted a low level of religious observance. Many regard themselves as doing God a favour if they even make church on Sundays.

It is not of importance whether the Eucharist is celebrated with pomp and ceremony or very simply. There is a place both for a service with beautiful music in a cathedral and a house Mass round a table in a kitchen. We all have different temperaments and a different aesthetic sense, which tend to make us prefer one kind of setting to another. But these are personal factors and do not go to the heart of the matter. The maximum of variety in celebration of the Eucharist should be allowed. What matters is the fact that, whether it is at a quiet 8 a.m. service or round a table in a house or with a superb choir in a cathedral, Christ himself is present feeding us with his own divine life.

Questions for discussion

1 Discuss some of the implications of having a 'sacramental' view of life.

2 Discuss the different ways in which Christ is present at the Eucharist.

3 How often do you think it is desirable that a person should receive Holy Communion?

4 Explore some of the things that Christians of different Churches now agree on about the Eucharist.

9

Following Christ

The Christian life is one of recognition and response. God has revealed his love for us in Jesus and, recognising this, we desire to respond to it with all that we have and are. This is the first characteristic of a Christian life-style — the attempt to offer ourselves completely, without any holding back, to Christ. We try to make ourselves totally available to God in prayer, in worship and in personal discipleship. The first two have been considered. We now come to the third.

GOD AND SELF

Most of what we do is motivated by self interest. This is good. It is how God made us. If a baby did not exert itself to get food when it was hungry it would not survive. If the human race had not got a strong desire to look after itself (which often means looking after itself at the expense of other creatures) it would not have evolved. This does not mean that the human race has achieved its dominant position only because it is more aggressive and ruthless than other creatures. Love, the desire to help and protect other members of the species, has been just as important a factor in our evolution as aggression. Nevertheless we have a strong tendency to assert our own interests against those of other people; and this cannot be wholly bad, for if we had not been made like this we would not be here. The Christian life, however, calls us to die and be re-born. We are called to love God and our neighbour.

The attempt to transcend our innate self-concern in a genuine love for God and others involves us in a continuing struggle. What we are struggling against varies depending on our temperament, condition of life and stage of Christian growth. According to Freud, human beings are motivated by a desire to maximise pleasure and minimise pain. (There is nothing in itself wrong with this.) So there is likely to be an element of pleasure seeking and pain avoiding in all we do. According to Adler we are driven by a desire to dominate others, a will to power. This, again, is likely to be present throughout our life. But, clearly, we all go through different stages of both physical and spiritual growth and our main temptation will vary accordingly. In T. S. Eliot's play *Murder in the Cathedral* Thomas a Becket says:

> The natural vigour in the venial sin
> Is the way in which our lives begin.
> Thirty years ago, I searched all the ways
> That lead to pleasure, advancement and praise.
> Delight in sense, in learning and in thought,
> Music and philosophy, curiosity,
> The purple bullfinch in the lilac tree,
> The tiltyard skill, the strategy of chess,
> Love in the garden, singing to the instrument,
> Were all things equally desirable.
> Ambition comes when early force is spent
> And when we find no longer all things possible.
> Ambition comes behind and unobservable.
> Sin grows with doing good.

Our lives begin with a natural vigour in the venial sin. Ambition comes when early force is spent. But this is not the end. If a person develops a stronger desire to serve God the temptations become trickier and harder.

Servant of God has chance of greater sin
And sorrow, than the man who serves a king
For those who serve the greater cause may make
the cause serve them.

Everyone has his or her own struggle, and what they are wrestling with depends on age and how far they have developed in the Christian life. But the main temptation will always be to keep some aspect of oneself for one's self, something unsurrendered to the Lord. There is a kingdom in every soul where we fly the flag of self and resist God. But never in the Christian life can we say, 'So far and no further'. Christ told a parable likening our relationship with God to that of a servant and master. When the servant comes in from the fields he does not *expect* to hear his master inviting him to have supper. He expects rather to be asked to get his master's supper, 'So you also, when you have done all that is commanded you, say "We are unworthy servants; we have only done what was our duty." ' (Luke 17. 7-10.) This call to surrender all that we have and are to God, to make ourselves available to him without anything held back, sounds inhuman. The way it has sometimes been put makes God appear to be an endlessly exacting tyrant. If this is how God appears to us then it is likely to be a reflection of our own super-ego rather than the God and Father of our Lord Jesus Christ.

We need to remind ourselves of three things:

First, this desire to offer ourselves totally to God is a response of love to his love for us. It is the same situation as occurs in a marriage service when two people, because they love each other, say that they will take each other 'for better for worse, for richer for poorer, in sickness and in health, to love and to cherish, till death us do part'. It is the nature of love to make unconditional affirmations. When two people fall in love they say such wild things as 'Darling, I will love you for ever.' The marriage service puts this unconditional affirmation in beautiful but down to earth language. The Christian in relationship to God is in the same situation. We make an unconditional response to God's unconditional love for us.

Second, according to Christian experience and understanding our nature is such that we find our true joy and freedom by making ourselves over completely to God, 'whose service is perfect freedom'. This is a familiar phrase in Christian prayers. This liberation is not a result of giving up responsibility for our own lives. The situation is very different from that when someone finds relief from the burden of freedom by giving themselves over to a Fuhrer figure or by living for a political party, though even here there is some pointer to man's true nature. For we are haunted by the absolute, by a sense that there is something which asks our total allegiance; and when a person gives it to another human being or a human cause, whether that cause is making money or changing the world, this is at once idolatory (which is giving one's total allegiance to what is less than God) and a pointer to God; for there is that within us which seeks the true object of worship. But when a person makes himself or herself available to God, this is not an escape from the pain and dilemma of being human. We still have to pray and wrestle and decide about all the various concerns of our life, but because our allegiance has been given to where it truly belongs, we find that peace, freedom and joy which can come from God and from God alone.

Third, once we have yielded Christ our allegiance and allowed him to be sovereign over the part of our lives that we have been withholding from him, then not only does this bring peace but God gives all that we are and have back to us for use in a new way.

The claim which God's love makes on us is not one claim alongside others — as though we had a duty to our family, our friends, our job and God all on the same plane. Our duty to God is of a different order and it comes to be expressed in and through our other duties. For example, if we make our money available to God it means in practice working out in an open and prayerful way how we meet the various financial claims upon us, from that of the Church and our family at one end to our personal pleasure at the other. God's claim upon our money is not identical with any one of these (not even that of the Church) but can come to be expressed in and through them all.

The first area to make available to God is our job. This needs saying, if only to contradict the widely held view that religious claims arise only in relation to what we do with our leisure time. For most men and women the best hours of each day, for the best years of their life, are given to working. This work, whether it is bringing up one's children or being a politician, is central to the lives of most people and therefore needs to be offered to God.

This immediately poses the question whether all jobs can be seen in Christian terms, for it is the job itself which is of prime importance, not any opportunities it might or might not offer to influence one's workmates. We need to be able to offer to God our bricklaying or engineering, our accountancy or writing skills, in the firm conviction that he can and will work in and through these activities for the building of his kingdom. When a person first becomes a Christian or when they first begin to think seriously in a Christian way about this side of their life, they often question whether they would not be serving God better by doing full-time church work. It is quite right that this question should occur. For we need to be open to any possibility. God might call us to be a priest or nun, to work abroad as a Christian agriculturalist, to retrain as a nurse, or to do anything. When Graham Greene went for instruction in the Christian faith the priest who instructed him revealed that he had once been an actor on the West End stage. Graham Greene wrote in his autobiography that this story came like a warning hand placed on his shoulder. 'See the danger of going too far.' That was the menace the story contained. 'Be very careful. Keep well within your depth. There are dangerous currents out at sea which could sweep you anywhere . . .' When baptised he felt sombre. 'Now the land had given way under my feet and I was afraid where the tide would take me. Even my marriage seemed uncertain to me now. Suppose I discovered in myself what Father Trollop had once discovered, the desire to be a priest . . . at that moment it seemed by no means impossible . . .' That last line is important. For Graham Greene realised that when our faith is strong we are aware that the tide of God's providence might indeed take us anywhere, perhaps well out of our depth.

Nevertheless, most Christians come to the conclusion that their vocation is to stay in their job as teacher or carpenter or whatever. Such secular jobs are just as much a calling as being a priest or a missionary doctor. When Martin Luther posed the question of what Christians should do he said that any job that was necessary to keep society going could be done by Christians. So if the job meets a human need, if it is necessary for the fabric of human society, it may be done. Sometimes a Christian may feel it is right to stay in a particular job, not because the job itself is worthwhile but for other reasons, e.g. someone may work on a conveyor belt in a factory because it is the only way of earning a living. This does not mean that there are no problems. Far from it. A thoughtful Christian working for a mining corporation in South Africa came to question the whole basis of what he was doing – the injustice of low wages, the immorality of apartheid, being part of the capitalist system which made use of and even reinforced all this. Such dilemmas arise in every society, especially our own. For example, should a Christian continue to work in the tobacco industry, or for an advertising agency which handles the account of a cigarette manufacturer? Whether a person, once they have had these questions raised can remain in such a job depends upon the answers to political questions as well, which are considered in the next chapter. The short answer is that, whether one is working as a Christian accountant in the West or a Christian bricklayer in Moscow, we cannot avoid compromising with the system. It is not possible in this world to keep one's hand completely clean. We will always be part of a social and political system that is less than perfect. If we try to withdraw and set up a utopian community we will still remain to some extent part of the rest of the world and dependent upon it.

Apart from our jobs we are conscious of other claims upon us; claims of the Church, of the family, of the local community, of the wider community both national and international. Anyone who is sensitive to the needs of the Church and the world will often be beset by feelings of burden and guilt. There is so much to do – am I doing enough? It is therefore important to approach this subject in a way which is both genuine and realistic, bearing in mind that we have only a limited amount of time and energy, but we do have some. Further, there are different gifts and vocations. We cannot be well informed on every subject or make a contribution to every one of the manifold problems of the world! But there may be one area in which we feel a particular concern and in which we could make a small contribution.

One person, when considering the claims upon him, might feel that because he has a particular interest in folk music his main (though not sole) contribution to the life of the local church will be running a Christian folk group; at the same time his main contribution to the local community will be by doing some occasional driving for the local good neighbourhood service; and his main concern with the wider world will be development and trying in various ways to educate young people to the real needs of the poorer nations. Christians should be aware of the many claims upon them, but this does not mean that they should take an active part in meeting all those claims, as our circumstances and our vocations are different. One person might choose to spend three evenings a week on church work. Another person might feel that her Christian commitment is best expressed by helping local children learn English. One person may be tied six nights a week looking after elderly parents or children, another person may have no ties except a too hectic social life (though hospitality is of course a proper Christian work). There are always dangers to be guarded against. The first is to think that we are already as fully committed as we can be. We may be; but it is a human tendency to let ourselves off too easily, or to get our priorities wrong. The second, if we are involved with the Church or community work, is to feel resentful towards others who do not seem as active as we are. We need to remind ourselves that each person has his own particular gift or vocation, her own particular ways of serving Christ. We have to do what we know is right for us and trust God that he will lead others to serve him in a way which is right for them. For some there is a third danger, that of overdoing it.

Such people have to learn to say 'No' to further commitments.

We offer our time and energy to God. We also offer our money. The Jews of old, and some Christians today, believe that the first ten per cent of a person's income should be offered to God for the work of religion and the relief of human need. This is not because such work is more important than the maintenance of our own families. It is not. It is a sign of our commitment to God, in particular a sign that all our money, whether it is spent on our family, ourselves, a favourite cause or the Church, is available for him, put to use in his service. Most churches today have a stewardship scheme whereby members are asked to think about how they use time, abilities and their money. They are invited to offer what they have to God and to promise some percentage of their income each year for the work of Christ in his Church.

There is a proper place for our own wants and interests when considering what to do with our time and energy and money. Many people assume that a Christian should never think of himself. In fact, of course, we do think of ourselves most of the time and this leads to unproductive guilt. If a person takes into account the proper place of self-interest, under God, then freed from guilt he is more likely to be able to give of himself to others. It is easy to see that self-interest has a place in the Christian life. First, imagine a person who tries always to think of others and never spends anything on himself. Taken to extremes this would mean old, even ragged clothes. It might mean such a narrowing of interests that the person would actually have nothing to bring to his relationships. For this reason alone, for the sake of other people, one has to think of oneself. For the sake of others we need to be moderately pleasing to the eye. For the sake of others we need to have some interests, some zest for life, to share with them. Second, if God cares about us, as he does, we have a duty to care for ourselves. If we have a genuine and proper love for ourselves we will be more, not less, likely to love others. God wants me, just as much as he wants other people, to develop the potential I have within me. He wants me to grow into being a full human being. This can only be done through having an interest in life. In this way our personality grows and we actually have something to bring to our relationships with God and other people. We cannot offer ourselves to God unless we have a self to offer, and that self will be one which has likes and dislikes, interests and passions. Monks and nuns (even members of contemplative orders) are usually very well informed about the world and often have a greater zest for life than other people.

In one Anglican Eucharist, (Rite A) after receiving communion, everyone can say 'We offer you our souls and bodies to be a living sacrifice. Send us out in the power of your spirit to live and work to your praise and glory'. This will involve us in thought and prayer. Thought and prayer about what job we should do, bearing in mind our particular abilities and interests and the needs of the world; about how we should spend our time and energy and money, about how we should balance the relative claims upon us of our family and friends, the Church and the whole community. The offering we make to God is both a duty and a joy. The pagan in us oscillates wildly between indulging ourselves and our pleasures without thought, and duty resentfully done. Under God what we regard as pleasure and what we regard as a chore can both be grasped with joy − for they are both means whereby we love God, love others, and ourselves grow into the person love desires us to become.

Much of the Christian life is a struggle between what we want for ourselves and the claim of love. *But not all.* At some moments, in some relationships. we genuinely want what love requires of us. We truly want the good of our wife or child or friend; at that moment it is the strongest element in our make-up. Such times suggest to us that in the end, or at the deepest level of our being, love is something natural to us. And so it is. For love is natural to God and we are made in his image. God does not have to struggle against his own selfish desires. He purely and perfectly wants our good with the whole of his divine being. People sometimes get depressed at the lack of love in the world and Christian community. They get even more depressed when they begin to realise how little love there is within themselves. However much truth there is in this realisation it is not the last word about our nature. For we are made in God's image with the potentiality to become as he is, and in our deepest moments we experience something of the naturalness of love. Edwin Muir wrote in one of his poems:

> Now in this iron reign
> I sing the liberty
> where each asks from each
> what each most wants to give,
> and each wakes in each
> what else would never be
> summoning so the rare
> Spirit to breathe and live.

The naturalness and yet the difficulty of love immediately underlines the need for grace, God's inspiration and strength. First, in the struggle between our own inclinations of lust, pride, ambition, greed, sloth, envy or whatever and the claim of love, we need grace to enable us to do what in our better moments we know we ought to do. Second we need grace so that what we ought to do becomes more and more natural to us. We need grace not just for individual decisions, but to obtain transformed being; so that loving decisions arise naturally for us; so that without thinking about it we have at the forefront of our mind the question, 'What would be the best for that person?'

Grace comes to us in many unexpected and undeserved ways. But Christian discipleship involves trying to live close to God in prayer and love. Then when we call upon him for illumination as to what is his will for us, or strength to do something difficult, we discover his help. This is the experience of millions of Christians in every age and culture. An old lady had to look after another old lady who had been incapacitated by a stroke. Time and again she felt she just could not go on. But she prayed and, as she said, each time she found the strength to do what she knew had to be done.

God's grace is essential; indeed without it there is no Christian life. For the Christian life begins and ends with a sense that without God we can do nothing and that with him all things are possible. What cuts us off from God is the feeling that we can do something off our own bat; our self satisfaction and complacency. However, the Christian life is not a question of pushing our nature beyond its natural limits. When a person is first converted or when he begins to take the Christian life seriously, it is easy to think that we can become quite good in a short time. It rapidly becomes obvious that this is not happening. What does sometimes happen, though, is that through grace, certain besetting weaknesses are less apparent and we are given new foes to fight. For the Christian, a good action is one which God has initiated and given him the strength to carry through. Therefore timing is all. God asks particular things of us at particular times and offers us the grace to do those things and not others. It is a question of being sensitive and receptive to what God wants of us, particularly to the point when he is calling us on to something else. God calls us to new tasks and to new possibilities of growth within ourselves. The sin is to resist this call. Jung found that many of his patients were middle aged — and that their problems were fundamentally spiritual. In the first part of their life they had been busy leading an outward life, building homes and pursuing careers. In middle age the neglected inner spiritual side started to push through, causing a disturbance in the psyche. We need to be sensitive to all the points of growth in our lives and not just the mid-life crisis. Retirement and old age is another crucial period. One Christian lady, who was very active in the church where on innumerable committees joined another church where she could, in her last years, concentrate more on the spiritual side of the Christian life, like attending daily services. How wise she was. She recognised the call to a new stage and responded. (What she did not quite realise was the strength of our inclination to be on things, and before long she had got herself elected to the council of the new church!)

A familiar problem for all of us is, how do we treat a person we do not like? We think, as a Christian, that we ought to like them, but we do not, and as a result we feel guilty. There is, however, no reason to feel guilty because we dislike someone. We cannot help our feelings. But we are quite right to realise that we are asked to love that person. Christian love is all-embracing, 'Love your enemy'. Christian love does not mean liking the person, but having a steady goodwill towards him. How do we achieve this? Grace and grace alone. So we need to pray. Our prayer will have at least five aspects. First, asking ourselves before God why we dislike that person. Have they really got horrible qualities which I have the right to shudder at; and, if so, is there something in myself, sparked off by them, that I have not recognised? Often we dislike things in other people that lie dormant and unrecognised within us. Second, that person too is a child of God and will have something of God in him. At a funeral service people always find something nice to say about the deceased. We do not have to wait till death to do this. Third, we can ask God for strength to do what we know needs doing. This does not mean pretence. It is best to begin our prayers with ruthless honesty. 'God, I hate that person, they really get on my nerves with their self centredness and their self pity.' But continue by thanking God for the qualities we can respect in them and just pray for them and/or a relationship with them. Fourth, we can trust that God will answer our prayer in ways expected and unexpected. Being a Christian does not mean that we have to pretend to feel kind when we do not feel it; it does not mean smiling politely when we are full of murderous aggression. We may have to do that quite a lot because it is civilised or prudent, but following Christ goes deeper than this. Sometimes the Christian thing will be to have it out with a person in a painful confrontation, being honest with them in as constructive a way as possible. Through bringing a person we don't like before God in this way it is possible to see how we can be both real (God does not want a pious fraud) and a follower of Christ. We can experience grace at work.

Questions for discussion

1 Do you agree that self-interest is a good thing? If so, how do you relate it to the claims of other people and God upon us?

2 How do you relate your job to your beliefs?

3 What do you find most difficult about trying to follow Christ?

4 Have you ever been conscious of receiving God's grace or help?

10

Love and Politics

It was said of one well known Cabinet Minister of recent times that his Christianity took the form of being kind to the Cabinet office cat. Being kind to the cat is admirable but what about the issues he debated day by day, the central concerns of his life? Did not the Christian faith, in which he professed to believe, have something to offer there? The Cabinet Minister is one of many who think that the Christian faith should confine itself to what goes on in the heart and to personal relationships. It should not, according to them, take sides on controversial political issues.

In order to see the integral connection between Christian discipleship and caring about the political order it is not necessary to dream up some new theology. The connection arises quite naturally out of the second commandment. We are told to love our neighbour as ourselves. That neighbour is part of society and will be affected, for good and ill, by social forces and political decisions. If you discover that an old person living nearby is not having her dustbins emptied regularly, it means ringing up the town hall. If there is no change for the better and the problem is widespread, it means making the matter a political issue. It involves getting one party or a group of politicians to take the matter seriously, to look into the causes and propose a remedy. What is true locally applies at national and international levels. If you are worried about the quality of education, it means raising questions about the educational budget and priorities of national spending. If you care about the developing world, it means raising questions about terms of trade between the rich and the poor countries. It is not possible to love our neighbour without being drawn into the political arena. If there ever was a time when Christian love for neighbour could be expressed simply in person to person terms or by founding some new institution like a school or hospital, this is no longer the case. As the historian A. J. P. Taylor has written, 'Until 1914 a sensible law abiding Englishman could pass through life and hardly notice the existence of the state, beyond the Post Office and the policeman. All this was changed by the impact of the Great War.' For good or ill the state now shapes much of our lives and it has moved into areas which were once the traditional preserve of the Churches. As one historian, who is critical of the Church's involvement with politics has written: 'These incursions make it very difficult for the Church *not* to be politically involved, for politics has actually moved into the Church's sphere.'

Loving Christian action and political action often seem to belong to two different worlds, the one gentle, the other aggressive; the one open, the other devious. Christian love leads me to listen with sympathy and sensitivity to a person who has just lost her husband. Political concern leads me to put a tough question at a rowdy meeting, a question to which others respond with rudeness and heckling. In fact, honest Christian love and political action belong together. Political action aims to create a certain kind of society, a society characterised by particular values, the value of justice for example. These values are also the concern of love, for loving someone means caring about their needs. Justice is concerned with the needs which all people have in common. Love is also concerned about these and, in addition, with those needs that are unique to every individual. We all need shelter, essential medical

141

care and nourishment. Love meets these needs by working for a just society in which every member has a right to shared provision. But we also have individual needs, for companionship or books or football or whist or bingo. Love is also concerned about these and will meet them through individual action. For example it might mean introducing a lonely old person to a club where whist is played two nights a week. Love and justice are not opposed, love includes and expresses itself through justice. And justice is the special concern of the political order. Thus, as has been said, 'the political expression of love is justice.'

In the well known parable the good Samaritan saw a human need and took steps to meet it. He picked up the battered traveller, treated him so far as he could, and took him to an inn to be looked after. If he became aware that travellers on that road are always likely to be attacked by brigands, love would lead him to get the road better policed. In a democratic society this would mean ensuring that the issue of an adequate police force was a concern of the political parties. If, on further looking into the matter, he came to the conclusion that the country was infested by brigands because of widespread poverty, illiteracy and unemployment, Christian love would lead him to work for the elimination of these ills, which again in a modern society would mainly have to be done through political processes. In the modern world Christian love is political or it is not love but sentimentalism.

It is natural that when a Christian seeks to serve his Lord in the political order he should ask which political ideology is closest to the mind of Christ. It is also understandable that Marxism offers an initial appeal to so many. Marxism has the concept of 'alienation', which appears to be an expression in the economic order of the Christian understanding of man as a sinner. Marxism also provides an attractive vision of the future, a classless society in which the creative potential in every individual will find fulfilment. It also suggests some of the steps which must be taken in order to achieve that society. In short, it offers a plausible analysis of human ills together with vision, hope and moral appeal. For it is one of the paradoxes of Marxism that, although on its own analysis moral values have no independent validity, it makes its way into the human heart through a powerful moral attraction. Indeed anyone who does not feel its moral, indeed religious, appeal (it has rightly been called a Jewish heresy) does not understand the world in which we live. Nevertheless Marxism, even apart from its horrifying record in practice (in Russia, between 1936 and 1938 alone, seven million people disappeared, of whom ninety per cent perished) is gravely defective at the heart of its theory. Two defects are singled out here. First, according to Marxist theory history consists of a series of economic revolutions from agrarian society through to a perfect communist society, via bourgeois and socialist revolutions. This process is literally inevitable, and moral evaluations of what is happening have no place. Moral values are only expressions of class interest. According to the Christian understanding of man, however, man is both free and capable of distinguishing good and evil. In the last analysis, however conditioned they may be by class interest, moral values have an objective validity and a life independent of the social forces in which they are championed and debated. We can say about a particular society, whether it is communist or socialist or capitalist, that it denies certain values, liberty perhaps or social justice. This critique will not inevitably be an expression of the class interest of the person who gives it. There is unlikely to be an element of objective truth present.

Another fatal flaw in the Marxist understanding of

man and society is in its view of the state. British and American children are brought up on the idea that the state is a neutral entity existing impartially for the benefit of all citizens. Marxism says that the state, far from being neutral, is the means used by a particular class to further its own interests. Marx wrote that 'the executive of the modern state is but a committee for managing the common affairs of the bourgeoisie', and again, 'the state is an organisation of violence for the suppression of some class'. The state is never neutral. In a bourgeois state it expresses bourgeois interests. In a socialist society it furthers the interests of the workers. The workers seize the apparatus of the state and make it serve their cause. In a perfect communist society the state will just wither away, but until then it is necessary for there to be a workers' state. This aspect of Marxist theory found its practical exponent in Lenin, who through a combination of luck and ruthlessness turned Russia into a one party workers' state along these lines. All opposition was ruthlessly suppressed.

This view of the state at once raises two questions. First, how is the transition to be made between the workers' state with its tight central control and the withering away of the state altogether? It is not conceivable that a group of people in power will voluntarily give it up completely. Second, in a pre-communist society, when men are not perfected, what happens if evil men obtain power? How can they be checked or ousted? Or assume that they are not evil men but the ordinary mixture of fear and pride, self interest and altruism as the rest of us. What happens if such people obtain absolute power and there is no way in which they can be stopped from carrying on policies that the majority of the citizens regard as mistaken?

Communism is not dangerous because those who run communist states are worse than the rest of us. They are not. The danger is that built into Marxist ideology

144

is the justification for a group of people thinking of themselves as representatives of the working class to take and hold on to absolute power. This is not the tyranny of a bad man who manages to gain power but a tyranny which justifies itself in ideological terms.

The main alternative to Marxism in the west is liberal democracy. Communist countries call themselves democratic but the main requirement of democracy is not present. For the essential requirement of democracy is that people should be able to replace one government by another of their choice through peaceful means. Thoughtful Marxists are very concerned about how Marxism can be made more democratic. They want Marxism expressed in such a way that certain democratic rights are preserved. But, however much Marxism may be revised or reformed, the idea of replacing one party by another, which is central to liberal democracy, is alien to communist theory and practice. Democracy as it is practised in the capitalist world is far from perfect; nevertheless, it expresses two insights which are central to the Christian understanding of man and society. First, it witnesses to the worth of every individual. In a democratic society each person has one vote and only one. One counts for one, whether a person is rich or poor, educated or uneducated. An important influence in the development of English democracy were the debates of Cromwell's army in Putney Parish Church in 1647. It was there that Colonel Rainsborough said, 'For really I think that the poorest he that is in England hath a life to live, as the greatest he; and therefore truly Sir, I think it is clear, that every man that is to live under a government ought first by his own consent to put himself under that government.'

This belief in the equal worth of every person is rooted in the Christian view of man as of worth in the eyes of God. Each one of us is unique, with different characteristics and qualities that are cherished by God. But, however different we are, God does not have favourites. We are all, equally, objects of his care. Closely linked with equality is liberty. These two values, though they sometimes work against each other in practise (for example, economic freedom leads to inequalities of wealth) are in fact integrally linked. It is because each person is of equal worth that the choices they make are given equal weight and they are given the maximum freedom to choose. Instead of one person or class or party imposing its choices on everyone else, each person, being treated equally, is given equal freedom of choice.

In an Islamic society the idea of the good life revealed in the Koran is built into every aspect of life. In contrast with this, there are the liberal democracies of the West. Are these liberal democracies to be regarded as essentially secular? They may be secular in the sense that no one religion or way of life is imposed upon all citizens, but they are not totally neutral as far as values are concerned. They are based upon a belief in the equal worth of each individual and this is rooted in the Christian understanding of the supreme value of each person in the eyes of God. Freedom is also rooted in the Christian view of man. For God gives man freedom and leaves him free even when he makes destructive choices. So, even though liberal democracies do not impose any one religion but leave people to follow their own beliefs, such societies are not value free. They are based upon the Christian view of each individual's worth. This does not mean that non-Christians cannot share this understanding of man's value and the consequent importance of democracy. They can and do. But this fact too is congruous with the Christian faith, for it affirms that certain basic values of both private and public morality can be glimpsed by all men whatever their beliefs.

Liberal democracies are rooted in the sense of each individual's value. They also reflect a recognition of how easy it is for even the best intentioned people to bring suffering to others. There is a strongly pessimistic strain in Christian thinking which has argued for the necessity of a strong state to keep man's sin in bounds. Martin Luther, for example, argued that each man had ten tyrants within him, and the state acted like the bars of a cage keeping us from tearing one another apart. But, if the citizens of a state are liable to rend one another to pieces unless they are held in check, its rulers are just as likely to do so as well. And what is to stop them? For this reason it is just as important to have some way of stopping the power of rulers getting out of hand as it is to have rulers at all. So it is that in a democracy there are three branches of government, with a measure of independence from one another, the executive, the legislature and the judiciary, and there are means of replacing one government with another if the people so wish it. The pessimistic tradition within Christian thought has always been used to justify the existence of strong governments. It was Reinhold Niebuhr who argued that this pessimistic view of man points just as strongly to the need for checks and balances on the powers of rulers and hence to a Christian justification for liberal democracy.

The Christian justification of democracy is based both on man's worth and man's tendency to corrupt even what is good. As Reinhold Niebuhr put it: 'Man's capacity for justice makes democracy possible; but man's inclination to injustice makes democracy necessary.' Democracy as we know it is badly flawed. Its saving grace, compared with communist states is that it has safeguards against tyranny whereas they build the possibility, and indeed the inevitability, of tyranny into the system. Democracy, is, as Niebuhr put

147

it, the worst possible form of government − except for every other.

These arguments indicating the underlying Christian basis of liberal democracy need to be qualified in a number of ways. First, democracy in the West is the result of a long historical process. Developing nations will not always be able to achieve a strong democratic system without intervening stages that fall far short of the ideal. Second, democracy may depend not only on shared values but on a degree of wealth-security. It is in Japan, one of the wealthiest countries in the world, that there has been the most successful transplantation of liberal democracy. Third, even in the one-party governments of some African countries there may be some expression of the democratic spirit appropriate to a more communal society. There may, for example, be a chance of participating in the decision-making process at village level. Further, even with a one-party government there may be some opportunity to elect or reject particular ministers. Fourth, though, as has been argued, there is something of permanent validity about liberal democracy, the form in which we know it is far from the last word. History has not stopped, and if democracy survives at all (and in a world of tyrannies it is a fragile plant) there will inevitably be development of one kind or another.

POWER

Reflection on Marxism and democracy points up the need to have an adequate understanding of the role of power in human life. Christians have sometimes thought that the world can be made better through education and persuasion alone. But crucial though these forces are, they are not enough by themselves. I can go to my next door neighbour and persuade him to contribute to some neighbourhood project. But if I go to a local industrial concern the situation is different. Industry by its very nature is organised to promote its own interests. Though it might donate relatively small amounts from its profits to charitable causes, and though it may deem it in its long term interests to co-operate with the community as a whole, it cannot deviate very far from pursuing its own goals. An individual human being might in extreme circumstances risk his life for someone else, diving into a river to save a child for example. It is contrary to the whole *raison d'etre* of a factory or a trade union or a nation or any other organised grouping to sacrifice itself totally for any other group. This means that, in relationships between groups of people, we cannot depend on persuasion alone and it is desirable to achieve some parity of power between them. This is for both a negative and a positive reason. The negative reason is that if there is a rough equality of power one group is less likely to tyrannise the other one. The positive reason is that it belongs to the dignity and worth of human beings that they have such power as will prevent others using them as a doormat.

If I meet a giant in the road, however good he is, he may be tempted either to bully or patronise me. But if I am the same size there is the likelihood of mutual respect. If the giant has a strong tendency to bully, then it is not just desirable but essential that the creatures he meets on the way are such as will compel his respect, whether he feels benevolent or not. For this reason, it is important that over the last hundred years trade unions in England and America have achieved such power that they are a force to be reckoned with. Whether they have too much power now is another question altogether; the fact remains that it is good that people can no longer be fired at the whim of an owner. Likewise, it is not *wholly* bad that there is a 'balance of terror' between the super powers. However fraught with danger this situation is (and it is), and however much the incredible waste of resources which could be used for the developing world, it does ensure that there can be no easy conquest of one major nation by another. The super-powers are forced to be very careful, they have to respect their opponents.

Power, which in the widest sense simply means the capacity to get things done, is not evil. God is all powerful. We ourselves have power of one kind or another. If we did not we would not exist. But when there is an imbalance of power, power is always threatening even when the intentions of the powerful individual or group are ostensibly innocent. So, in the relationship between God and man, God becomes incarnate, and meets us as friend and brother. He deals with us at our level of power. It is the measure of the value we have in his eyes that he deals with us as equals. So the Christian approach to relationships between groups and nations, where the power factor is crucial, will be to try to achieve a rough equality of power. This is for the positive reason of imparting to people the dignity we recognise them to have by virtue of their status as human beings, and for the negative reason of preventing more powerful groups from exploiting others. So the Christian approach to the developing world will be to build up the power of the poorer nations, for example their economic self-sufficiency. Likewise with any subjugated group, for example, black people in South Africa. The Christian approach will not confine itself to kindness to individuals or to persuasion of the South African government. For the situation will change only when the power of the black people is recognised and accorded respect — political and economic power. Too often, alas, it is only when the power of physical violence is recognised that the first two are ceded.

If some people are unrealistic, thinking that manifestly unjust situations can be changed for the better simply by talk, others are too cynical in believing that the power factor alone is relevant in relationships between groups. In recent years the gap between the rich and the poor nations has widened and the terms of trade have worked increasingly against the developing world. But there is nothing inevitable about this, for the relationship between the Scandinavian countries and Holland on the one hand and the poorer nations on the other, has not followed the general pattern. No doubt the reasons for this are complex, including both political and moral factors. But as Professor Charles Elliott has suggested, relationships between nations and groups are like two oil tankers facing a head-on collision. There is not enough freedom of manoeuvre to go into reverse, but there is enough to avert a collision.

ORDER, FREEDOM, JUSTICE

The Christian will work for a world characterised by the values of order, freedom and justice. It is not necessary to be a Christian to see the validity and importance of these values, but they are nevertheless rooted in the Christian understanding of man and society.

There can be no human community without order, and in a world where human beings are liable to cheat, exploit and oppress their neighbours there has to be a final sanction of force to ensure that order is maintained. But two points need to be kept in mind. First, those who have the largest stake in the status quo are those most likely to champion the necessity of order rather than other values. The call for order, for more police, for a clamp down on this that and the other, is not quite so disinterested as some would like to think.

151

Second, a government that takes repressive measures in the name of order may not bring about order at all. A group of Dominicans in jail in Brazil a few years ago wrote, 'The regime's *raison d'etre* is national security, and the people have never been less secure; at any moment they can be victims of injustice, thrown into prison, put to death. Torture has become a normal means of government. No one can trust anyone else. There are spies everywhere.' A similar criticism can be made against communist countries. They give the impression of being ordered, certainly everything is controlled. But, as one person who escaped from behind the Iron Curtain said, 'It was literally impossible to have a friend.' You never knew who would betray you. True order gives people the security to live and plan their lives in a relaxed way. Tyrannical control by governments of the left or right is not order but repression.

The value of freedom arises out of the basic worth of, and respect due to, every human being made in the image of God. God made man free and Christ left people free even to crucify him. Such is the value that Christ places on freedom. But freedom in society is not an absolute, and nowadays we accept the loss of many freedoms that people once took for granted. For example, we are not free to buy ourselves commissions in the army or indeed to buy whole regiments, as people were not so long ago. It is not possible to have an ordered community life without some curtailment of liberty. We are not free, in England, to drive down the right hand side of the road or to fly an aeroplane under the bridges of London. But, where possible, individual freedoms should always be maximised, and certain liberties, freedom of speech, religion and assembly, for example, are basic to democracy.

A just society could be defined as one in which the basic needs of all members of the community are met.

You cannot read the Bible without hearing again and again God's concern for the poor and his anger against those who exploit them. This is the message of the great eighth century BC prophets, and, perhaps even more impressive, it is this moral insight which is enshrined in the early Hebrew legal codes of Exodus, Deuteronomy and Leviticus. Since John Locke in the seventeenth century, many people have thought that there is an absolute right to private property, 'the inherent sacredness of the breeches pocket'. Some early fathers of the Church would have found this very strange, for they taught that God had given the goods of the earth not to particular individuals but to mankind as a whole for everyone to share. Therefore, when money is given by the rich to the poor this is not an act of charity but a matter of justice. It is a question of justice not charity that the world as a whole should now be freed from the poverty which still afflicts over 650 million people.

The Marxist analysis of man and society is false. Or, rather, a finger is put on details of the truth in such a way as to smudge and distort the whole picture. One detail of the truth is the way the values we assert are likely to be conditioned by our experience of life. A man perched on a pile of logs that is swaying precariously calls out to people to keep things steady. He is conscious of how much he will be hurt if the pile breaks up and so he wants stability at all costs. A man squashed under the pile calls to be let out. He is hurt already and does not care about the break up of the pile; indeed it seems to him inevitable if he is going to extricate himself from the bottom. So it is that some call for order and others call for justice. Both values are necessary and neither are totally class determined, but the one we champion most fiercely is likely to be conditioned by our stake in the status quo. To one who believes in the incarnation, in the reality of God entering fully into our environment, the importance of a person's total situation in life is not surprising and will not be neglected.

The other detail of the truth is the Marxist stress on man as part of society. Within God there is both personhood and community. There are three persons in one Godhead. So individuality and society are not antagonistic. They enhance and reinforce one another. Man is made in the image of God. So, if in relation to communism it must be asserted that there can be no true society which does not allow the maximum freedom for individual flourishing, it must also be said about capitalism that there can be no individual well-being apart from the well-being of society as a whole. Concerning all freebooting individualism it has to be said that the individual belongs by his nature, by his very essence, to other people. In primitive societies people feel quite naturally part of the group. In the West people tend to feel essentially isolated from one another. Many emerge from their hideouts, if at all, to make only fleeting contact with other hooded passers by. This sense is unhealthy and false to the Christian understanding of man made in God's image. The individual and society are integrally linked.

DISCIPLESHIP AND THE POLITICAL ORDER

It is not possible to love our neighbour without caring about the society which so largely shapes him. The Lord is to be served not just in person-to-person situations but through striving to bring about just and economic structures. This does not mean a Marxist society. Communism is dangerous, not because it is atheistic, but because of its built-in tendency to tyranny. Liberal democracies, imperfect though they are, offer the best chance of avoiding tyranny and expressing the worth of every single human being. This worth is more likely to be recognised if each group within society, and each nation within the world as a whole, has enough power to cause it to be respected by other groups and nations. The power factor cannot be ignored both for positive and negative reasons. But values are equally important, and the Christian will seek to achieve an ordered society in which the basic needs of all human beings are met and individual liberties are cherished. There are a thousand problems and concerns, which are daily brought to our notice in the media, from the possibility of excessive lead in petrol damaging the health of children, to the necessity of arms reductions; from the preservation of trees to the need for irrigation schemes in desert areas. There are no simplistic solutions to these problems. There is no total solution. A wise Christian will be one who takes one or two of these concerns, tries to understand what is the best way to approach the problem and then takes such steps as are possible, including political action.

Man is part of society. As soon as we develop a concern about the political and economic forces of the society, forces which shape us much more than we realise, love becomes political. In this political order too, the Lord is to be loved and followed.

Questions for discussion

1   Examine, in relation to some specific issues, why it is that Christianity today must be expressed in political terms as well as personal ones.

2   Do you agree that liberal democracy can be justified in Christian terms?

3   What values are most dear to you? How far, if at all, do they reflect class bias or personal prejudice?

4   What political or social issue would you most like to make a contribution towards?

Epilogue

This book has sketched out the fundamentals of Christian belief with some attempt to meet the difficulties felt by many modern people. It has suggested that the Christian life is one of recognition and response; the response taking the form of prayer, eucharistic worship and a personal discipleship which has to be expressed in political terms as well as in intimate relationships. Yet in the end a book like this can convey only faintly the distinctive feel of Christianity. Perhaps this can only be done through the lives of authentic believers, whether in past ages or our own, or through certain novels and plays. If we want to know what it is to have a profoundly moral atheism it is no good reading a tedious atheistic tract. We read, say, the novels of Conrad. If we want to know what it is to rebel against the nature of things and to express this in a compassion for others, we read the novels of Camus. There are, thank God, Christian writings which convey just as powerfully what it is to have a Christian feel for life. What is revealed in them is a world apart from the banality and trite moralism, the anti-life mentality that still too often passes as Christianity. Dostoevsky's novels, for example, are able to convey the sense of what a Christian view of life is about. To take just one, in *Crime and Punishment* a man is trapped in horrendous sin and mental nightmare; but he is redeemed by a woman, who is herself caught up in sinful circumstances, because her love is grounded in God and God's providence. Patrick

White in *The Riders in the Chariot* or William Golding in *Darkness Visible*, to mention just two others, are able to communicate the sense that what is really happening in the events of our lives, and what is truly significant, is very different from what we think is happening and what we now judge to be important.

If this sense has to be summed up in one inadequate paragraph we must say it has to do with affirmation. Despite the tragedy and evil in life, despite the sin in others and oneself, despite the bleakness (well conveyed in the plays of Samuel Beckett), it is still possible to affirm life, to affirm others and to affirm oneself. It is possible to have, in a fine phrase of Paul Tillich, the courage to be.

This affirmation is not a desperate reaction to an underlying despair; it is not a reckless abandon flying out of a sense that nothing means anything. It is rooted in the conviction that the universe itself is affirmed by a sheer goodness who lives both beyond it and at the painful centre of our struggles. It is this that makes the affirmation Christian; and, to take one example, it emerges strongly in Pasternak's popular novel *Dr. Zhivago*. Zhivago comes to see Lara, the girl he loves, and his feelings are described in the words, 'O how sweet it was to be alive. How good to be alive and to love life! And how he longed to thank life, thank existence itself, directly, face to face, to thank life in person'. In the end Zhivago and Lara have to part, Zhivago dies and Lara goes to the house where his body lies. She reflects on what it was that drew them so close and even in her grief she is able to witness not just to the mystery of existence but to its ultimate worthwhileness. 'Never, never, not even in their moments of richest and wildest happiness, had they lost the sense of what is highest and most ravishing — joy in the whole universe, its form, its beauty, their feeling of their own belonging to it, being part of it.' In her desolation words of grief and affirmation come tumbling out: 'The way God brings us together, Oh, I can't bear it. O Lord, I cry and I cry. Your going that's the end of me. Again something big, inescapable. The riddle of life, the riddle of death, the beauty of genius, the beauty of loving that, yes, that we understood'.

Other Books from Winston Press

Bright Intervals
by James Bitney

Experiencing God All Ways and Every Day
by J. Norman King

God Present
by Georges Lefebvre

Faith in Jesus Christ
by John Coventry

Gospel Journey
by Ernest Ferlita

Kept Moments
by Gerhard E. Frost

Pilgrimage to Renewal
by Herb Brokering

Praying
by Robert Faricy

Our Story According to St. Mark
by William H. Barnwell

Songs of Suffering
by Nathan R. Kollar

The Breath of Life
by Ron DelBene

The Joy of the Psalms
by Herb and Mary Montgomery

The Winston Commentary on the Gospels
by Michael Fallon

Toward the Heart of God
by John Dalrymple